'SOUNDS ORIGINAL'

Keith Desmond

ATHENA PRESS
LONDON

'SOUNDS ORIGINAL'
Copyright Keith Desmond 2003

All Rights Reserved

No part of this book may be reproduced in any form
by photocopying or by any electronic or mechanical means,
including information storage or retrieval systems,
without permission in writing from both the copyright
owner and the publisher of this book.

ISBN 1 84401 122 4

First Published 2003 by
ATHENA PRESS
Queen's House, 2 Holly Road
Twickenham, TW1 4EG

Printed for Athena Press

'SOUNDS ORIGINAL'

With special thanks to Dr John Blanchard
and the Evangelical Press for kind permission to quote from
his books
Does God Believe in Atheists? and
Where Was God on September 11th?

For
Liz, Rhiannon, Adam
and
the grandchildren

Acknowledgments

A great deal of what follows would not be there without the continual encouragement of my family and more than a few friends.

After writing for eighteen months as memory and inspiration led, which were not always around when most required, I was pleased to receive a positive response from Athena Press who were willing to put their necks on the line with a first time author.

My warmest thanks go with love to Monique and Ron Truscott, Heather Wright and David Maloney who read vast portions of the manuscript with a discerning eye, infinite patience, and encouraged me to keep writing.

I realised that I needed to give the manuscript to someone who would read it with 'no messing' and let me know 'whose horse I thought I was on'. Naturally, it had to be someone from the north, and Sue Allen said 'She would have a go as long as I didn't mind strict discipline and a good slap as she saw fit'. My brother Andrew, who also doesn't take prisoners, was given some of the chapters to scrutinise. Sue was good to her word, and apart from pointing out that 'This bit doesn't make sense', and 'A sixty-seven word sentence, which also happened to be one paragraph, felt like heavy going', plus 'That chapter just stopped – you haven't finished it'. All of the above steered me through chapter and verse with a generous attitude couched in a smile, and I know the tales have improved from their help and scrutiny.

I do thank my wife for her love, patience and support, but I suppose mostly for her understanding – yes, definitely – her understanding.

Contents

Introduction	xi
From t'Mill to Soho	13
On Meeting David and The Teeth	17
'How Unlike the Home Life of Our Own Dear Queen'	20
Christmas in Lesotho	43
Roots of Africa	52
Blatant Name-dropping	
Elizabeth Taylor	66
HRH Princess Margaret	68
Carroll Baker	72
Ursula Andress	74
Others Best Not Mentioned	75
Sophia Loren	75
Billy Joel	75
Madonna	83
The *Kon-Tiki* Man and Tigris	88
Jairus Jiri – Zimbabwe	114
Death and Cricket	117
'Collar the Lot'	130
Situations Best Avoided	134
Boredom and Vultures	138

The Search for Lord Lucan	155
The Director – the PA – and the Tick	167
Eric Hebborn – 'Master Forger'	180
The Final Chapter	187
Sounds Personal	200

Introduction

'Didn't you have a run-in with Lord Lucan or something, and what about that thing with Princess Margaret and her hi-fi?'

I was asked the above question by a friend of mine a few years ago, who went on to suggest that I ought to write about the people I had met or worked with over the years. Another colleague agreed, and asked if I had kept any kind of journal when working in Africa or Thailand.

My eldest daughter, Liz, who had heard the tales many times, gave me much encouragement and told me, 'Don't forget to write about the snake and the tick.' I got the feeling she would like the stories to be in widescreen with surround sound.

I did point out to the enthusiasts, should it have slipped their memory, I was a film technician who recorded sound for TV documentaries, not a writer – although I had been known to read a book on a few occasions.

During some of the Millennium gatherings, friends who had been politely and patiently listening to my accounts of travel and derring-do, usually fuelled by some glasses of red wine, did mention it would be interesting to read some of the other tales, but unfortunately they didn't have time to listen to any right then. I made a 'furtive' gesture, spilling my wine, whilst pointing out my lack of literary experience.

A most glamorous lady, who did have time to listen, encouraged me some more. She reminded me that few people ever get to the locations or meet the remarkable characters I have had the good fortune to bump into in my line of work. Just tell the tale as it was: 'You don't have to blow the gaff.'

'Write them down, and see how they turn out,' suggested my wife.

In the past thirty-eight years I have worked on over a thousand different productions and very few of them are worth mentioning. Most kept the bank manager happy and eventually cleared the mortgage.

Some however, have been truly remarkable, quite amazing, and life-changing for many reasons. The crews I have worked with, the people I have met, and the outstanding places visited, provide lasting memories of immense riches and freedom.

The chapters that 'have turned out' hopefully offer a glimpse of the shafts of sunlight in my memory which brought pleasure, affection, emotion, excitement and humour during my working life.

From t'Mill to Soho

By 1962 my life had not yet turned the corner. It revolved around cricket, Sophia Loren, tennis, Elizabeth Taylor, music and Ursula Andress. Three of these I had a direct access to, the other three inclined more towards emotional turmoil, causing hours of wonderful thoughts and undiscovered passion.

I was a wages clerk at a mill in Bradford, Yorkshire.

Aged twenty-four, I saw a grand job advertised in a clerical journal, which I thought would suit me just fine. A company in London had recently been formed, and required an assistant accountant. Well, I wasn't an assistant accountant, I was a wages clerk with aspirations, but I had been attending night school for the past six years, hoping this would further promotion.

The reporters and producers on the BBC's *Panorama* had parted company. The reporters, along with some financial backers, had formed a film company called Television Reporters International Limited. I thought, That's a right mouthful, I'll have a crack at that. I loved the idea of telling my mates in the north I was working for Television Reporters International or TRI, as it was known for short. I tried to impress some girls at t'Locarno Ballroom on Manningham Lane, but they just said, 'Yer wot?'

After a brief pause, I made the mistake of justifying my crass stupidity by informing them that the 'T' stood for Television, and the 'I' for International, and I could well travel abroad, you know. One girl, a statuesque peroxide blonde with a formidable bust, looked me straight in the eye, and told me with colourful articulation, 'Yeah, you'll be bloody lucky if you mek it t'Isle o' Man!' After an intake of breath, and smarting ever so slightly, I backed away and thought, Well, so much for impressing the women of Bradford.'

The whole of this performance wouldn't have been so pathetic if I'd got the job, but at the time I hadn't even applied for it.

The thought of working in London had the added prospect

that I could bump into S Loren or E Taylor much more readily in Soho than in Bradford. As, by my reckoning, neither of them had ever been to Bradford.

I did apply, and I got the job. I never knew how, as my night school qualifications didn't take me to the level of assistant accountant. I could only think, Maybe it was that bit about the salary that did it. At the interview, I was wearing my best suit to impress, my shirt had a detachable stiff collar, and my cuffs could not have been cleaner.

The General Manager and Senior Accountant asked me how much I was expecting my salary to be. I thought, Well, that's right civil of them to ask. Whereas they thought, We've got a right lemon here. I mulled it over for a moment or two, and then remembered my English teacher had told me: 'Never mull, you look vacant when you mull.' I thought, best move from mull to 'consider' – the appearance of 'considering' would be more conducive. I didn't want them to think I didn't 'consider' things.

I knew the average man's salary at the time was about £900 per annum, and as I was earning £650 a year in t'mill I said, being cautious, 'I'd be happy with £850 per annum.'

It didn't strike me as odd then, but one of them said, 'Done,' and the other said, 'Good' – almost simultaneously. I had the feeling it had been cast in stone, and there was no going back.

On the way home to Bradford, I pondered on my good fortune in striking a deal which gave me £200 a year more than I was getting in t'mill, and if the average man's salary was £900 a year, I was only £50 quid short of becoming an 'average man'.

When I told my Auntie Ruth I was going to work in London for a television company, she just looked at me and said, 'Well, luv – I'll go t'foot of our stairs, – now don't you go becoming a pansy, you know what it's like down south.' She was genuinely pleased, which did surprise me, as my Dad, her older brother, had died seven years earlier, and Auntie Ruth always told me I had to look after my mother and brothers. Her farewell to me was to say, 'It's a good thing you're doing, cos if it's on't telly it must be true. After all, they'd never spend all that money on a programme if it weren't.'

It took me about twenty minutes working in TV to discover that Auntie Ruth was mistaken.

Some months later, I learned from Ann Moore, the General Manager's secretary, who can only be described as a completely lovely young woman, apparently they would have been prepared to pay me £1,100 a year, with a travel allowance. It never dawned on me that I would have to travel to work in London; I'd always walked t'mill.

It was a good learning curve.

Ludovic Kennedy, Robert Kee, Malcolm Muggeridge, and James Mossman were the reporters who had left *Panorama* to form TRI.

These four were at the top of the Premier League in their day, and were among the best the country had in television journalism. The producers and accountants at the BBC were trying to tell these journalists how to make television documentaries. Naturally they left.

For me, it was like discovering Shangri-la. I learnt much about TV journalism, particularly from Ludovic Kennedy and Malcolm Muggeridge. They were always willing to help in any way they could. I knew that they were good, but it's only with thirty-eight years' hindsight that I now know just how good they were.

In the October of '62, when I arrived in Soho, the leading contenders in the news were Christine Keeler, John Profumo MP, Dr Stephen Ward, Mandy Rice-Davies and others. Ludovic Kennedy was at the hub of the trial, and TRI was buzzing.

It did grab me that this was definitely a tad more energetic and exciting than paying the evening shift in Furnishing Fabrics.

After a year, things with TRI were beginning to wobble, the money men began to interfere, and ultimately hampered productions.

Whilst working in Wardour Street I had picked up a whole gamut of technical information about TV documentaries, most of all from Neville Druce and Michael Colomb. In January 1964 they formed a company called Better Sound (still operating today) and asked if I would join them to give them a hand with their accounts, and at the same time they would teach me the camera and sound side of the business. Neville was a sound research engineer who had come from the hallowed portals of the BBC at Kingswood Warren, and Michael had been a sound recordist for some fifteen years. Once more, I was in good company.

In the next twelve months I went out with Michael on many programmes, working as his sound assistant and boom swinger. They were usually short magazine slots of five to six minutes, but these were the beginnings.

One evening Michael and I had a very short job. It was a news slot for Italian Television. That evening was the premiere of the film *The Carpetbaggers* in Leicester Square, and we had been asked to interview Carroll Baker, the star of the film, at her hotel prior to her leaving for Leicester Square (for what happened next, see 'Blatant Name-dropping').

The documentaries in the late Sixties covered a wide variety of topics, from Victims of Thalidomide, Tea Ladies in Acton, Public Schools, to Flower Power in Hyde Park. It was a thorough grounding in the nuances of rapid TV documentaries. The BBC always had slots on *Nationwide* and *Today* that needed to be filled, and Better Sound got plenty of them. In 1972, however, considering there hadn't been a glimpse of E Taylor or S Loren, I bit the bullet, and went freelance.

On Meeting David and The Teeth

I first worked with the cameraman Martin Bell on a BBC *Blue Peter* film along with John Noakes and Peter Purvis. This can only be classed as name-dropping if you were born between 1961 and 1966. The programme featured a search for the Loch Ness Monster. The BBC at this time was – undoubtedly – *THE BEE BEE CEE*, and ruled the airwaves, as Britannia would only have expected.

On one occasion I recall a producer stating very loudly and clearly, 'But my dear fellow, one must understand, after all – we are *the BBC!*'

To my great relief Martin was not of that ilk, and we had a good shoot on Loch Ness.

Over the next few months I worked with Martin on a number of programmes for the mighty Corporation, and found him easy to be with. Added to this, he had the rare gift of being a 'listening cameraman' and always filmed around the dialogue containing essential content. Finding such a cameraman is like discovering gold.

David Graham was the camera assistant Martin usually chose to work with, and had done so for a number of years. As yet I still had to meet him, but I was assured that as camera assistants go, he had a good pedigree and a CV that carried with it… considerable envy.

The young David Graham had been through drama school and appeared in a number of premier feature films.

David always felt he had reached the zenith of his film career when he carried Robert Mitchum's bags from a taxi to a hotel foyer. At that time Robert Mitchum was one of the Hollywood greats and a recognised worldwide megastar, so for David to appear in the same film as R Mitchum was no small matter.

David was always man enough to admit that, in the movie, all you could see of him were his legs and feet – but they were his legs and his feet, he knew that, and his mother knew that. The bags were almost incidental.

Having reached the pinnacle of a career at such an early age, David joined British Airways as a flight attendant, and by all accounts was a jolly good flight attendant. As he recalled, they only had one death on his first flight, and one heart attack (not fatal). He felt this was unfortunate; it was his maiden outing with BA and knew he could not be held responsible in any way. Rumour has it that he did serve jolly splendid coffee, tea or milk.

On his second flight the captain aborted the take-off, just before committing the plane to going airborne. There was insufficient runway left and as the captain reversed the engines and applied the brakes, the plane trundled on to the grass at the end of the tarmac.

David felt that he should perhaps try other channels for a career – so he became a camera assistant.

This was the David I met one morning at a hotel in London where Tory MP Geoffrey Howe was to make some political declaration of allegiance to Prime Minister Ted Heath. Our brief was to film a short piece of the speech for *Panorama* and then to clear off.

David arrived at the hotel carrying more metal camera cases than is possible for an average human. He put the cases down and walked towards Martin and myself.

Martin went through the usual banter: 'David – Keith, Keith – David.'

David wasn't traditionally handsome, in the accepted male model package. He was more attractive – and certainly good-looking in a sort of rugged physical way. One could immediately see why he had been chosen to carry the bags of Robert Mitchum in a movie. He hadn't long been back from a job in Iran and still had a weathered tan. A Government Health Warning ought to have been given to the recipient of his smile, along with a pair of sunglasses. It wasn't that he had more teeth than anyone else, they were just larger, whiter, and perfectly even with no gaps. These were serious, uppercase TEETH. One felt a smile of that stature ought to be announced by a ringmaster with whip.

To be frank, I couldn't take my eyes off the smile. It was infectious. It made you feel good.

Added to this, he had appealing large brown eyes containing a mischievous gleam when the smile was around.

Was this love at first sight?

He also had hair; dark brown tousled hair. In fact he had a lot of hair, the kind of hair that always looks great no matter which way you have been laying on it.

I've always noticed men with hair.

At the time of meeting David, I didn't have much hair. It had been noticed, by some, that I had very little hair.

David came wrapped in designer blue jeans and a tasteful slim blue denim jacket – he looked good – oh, did he look good!

The next few months brought the three of us together on some short films for the BBC and my first experience of corporate work with IBM. A spot of good-natured bonding was achieved by us, and we began to work well together as a team. The humour we found in most situations always eased any untoward moments with directors and the like, and gave David's teeth the opportunity to slip into first gear and add a touch of healing warmth.

'How Unlike the Home Life of Our Own Dear Queen'

In July 1974, Martin, David and I set out for Africa. It was the first time for each of us, and we could never have realised how it would change our lives.

Survival Anglia had asked us to spend six weeks with Richard Leakey and his team at Lake Rudolf (now Lake Turkana) in northern Kenya. Our brief was to work with Leakey and his group of palaeontologists, geologists and zoologists to film the origins of early man at Lake Rudolf. The Leakey team had discovered a skull in 1972, which he had named '1470' and had decided was three-million-years-old. This caused a buzz of excitement in the scientific world, and it was that 'buzz' Survival Anglia wanted us to get on film.

The expedition was to start in Nairobi, and two days before we arrived four trucks had left with tents and everything needed to keep us alive for six weeks, in the centre of nowhere. The three-day journey from Nairobi to the Leakey camp, on the east of the lake at Koobi Fora, was being organised by the Kamba people, who were experts in getting equipment across impossible terrain.

We flew up to Lake Rudolf in a twin-prop Barron a couple of days later, and as we approached the southern shore of the lake, we couldn't help but notice the jewel like green of the water. Someone pointed out to us later that it was often referred to as the Jade Sea. From the plane window we could see nothing but barren landscape with mountains on the west side of the lake and wilderness on the east.

As we approached a dirt airstrip, we saw vast herds of zebra, oryx and topi moving slowly about chewing on desert grass.

We got out of the plane to be met by six attractive young ladies with wonderful suntans, some with American accents. David smiled, and the sun caught his teeth to maximum advantage. The smile had the desired effect; there was now no ice to be broken (not that there could be any ice in a temperature of 30°). The nice young ladies helped us unload our gear, which was kind of them, as we didn't know who they were. They were archaeologists who had finished studying with Richard Leakey and the team, and were now loading their gear into the Barron ready to fly back to Nairobi.

David's smile had 'What a shame!' written on it, and we said, 'Thank you, and farewell!'

Three Land Rovers were waiting to take us, and our equipment, on the half-hour drive, to the camp.

The tents had been pitched a short distance from the lakeside, and it looked the perfect location. A large tent was made ready for our equipment, and was fitted with a couple a generators. Most important was the mess tent, which had a table with eight camp chairs, a drinks table, and a fridge filled with soft drinks and some beer.

The necessary latrines had been set back from the camp by about fifty metres. These comprised a couple of single tents fitted with a plank of wood with a hole, and below – a 'long-drop'. Very efficient!

We were introduced to the Kamba men who would be looking after us. They pointed out the earth oven, which was a trench filled with hot coals that were never allowed to go out. This meant that within minutes cups of tea could be imminent. The Kamba man who appeared to be running all this was called Benson (as in Hedges) – we never knew why, and nobody could tell us, but he was extremely thorough and made wonderful tea.

Our token 'White Hunter' who ran the entire camp was a wild Irishman called Liam Linn. He had lived in Kenya many years and was said to be a crack shot. He would see that no harm came to any of us!

Forbes Taylor was our director from Survival Anglia. He had a good track record, was a pukka chap, and down to share a tent with me.

John Hemmingway was a likeable American who, as far as I can remember, was there to look after the Boston TV station WGBH's interest, and those of *National Geographic*. Plus he was very rich (but I don't see that is of any interest).

'How Unlike the Home Life of Our Own Dear Queen'

Bob Campbell the cameraman, who shot a wonderful film on gorillas with Dian Fossey in Rwanda was there to help us. This is the same Bob Campbell as portrayed by Brian Brown in the film *Gorillas in the Mist* – but to set the record straight, this Bob Campbell did not take a bath with either Dian Fossey or Sigourney Weaver, and what's more is better looking than Brian Brown.

The only person we hadn't met was Richard Leakey, who was thought to be out on a dig somewhere. His Cessna aircraft had apparently left the strip two hours earlier.

Over the evening meal, Bob told us the Shangilla tribesmen should be arriving the following day. About fifteen of these men had been asked if they would like to help us do some work. They hadn't been told what kind of work, as they didn't know what television was, and had no understanding of film. These were basic tribesmen, who lived near the Omo River in the north and would walk the seventy miles to be with us.

Bob then went on to inform us that part of their basic culture was the practice of castration if displeased. He went on to clarify the ritual saying, 'They don't just castrate you in cold blood, they kill you first, then castrate you so you are unaware of any pain.'

I can't say that brought comfort to any of us. He also mentioned that we would know if any of them had been practising the custom recently as they would be wearing the 'male jewels' around their necks.

Forbes suggested that we could do well to have early nights, as we would be starting at around 5 a.m. when the day is cooler and the light is better. Martin was all for this and said we should stop at 11 a.m. as the light was too 'toppy' at that time of day and we could start again at 3:30 p.m. till sunset.

At about 8:30 p.m. Forbes and I toddled off to our tent, with what must have been similar thoughts going through both our heads at the same time: Does he snore? Does he talk in his sleep? Does he *walk* in his sleep? Does he have queer leanings? I don't think 'gay' had been invented in 1974.

After an uneventful night, and what felt like a deep sleep, I turned over at 5 a.m. to discover Forbes had gone AWOL. I could hear Kamba voices talking quietly a short distance away, and small waves lapping on the lake shore. I had just woken sufficiently to sit up in bed and consider whether I should raise the alarm for our missing director, when the zip on the door flap to the tent opened and Forbes pushed his face into the tent and hissed loudly, 'Africa Screams!'

It turned out he had been awake for the last hour or so listening to my snoring, so he had got up for a chat with the Kamba who had made him a pot of tea, and would I like a cup?

I thought, I'm going to like it here!

At breakfast Forbes and John outlined the day, and told us we would know more when they had chatted to Richard. Liam gave us a few useful pointers about staying alive in the area. Should we come across any lions by chance, please, don't go annoying them, and best not pick up any snakes, no matter how pretty they look...

The sun was clipping the horizon, and we had just finished loading our equipment into a couple of weather worn Land Rovers, when we heard a vehicle approaching.

Richard Erskine Leakey had arrived.

I don't quite know what I was expecting in a palaeontologist whose discovery of a skull two years earlier had shaken the scientific world, but it was not that of a young man about twenty-nine or thirty, wearing a beret, and smoking a bent pipe.

We were introduced, in a polite manner, with each of us eying the other as if to begin a mating ritual.

Richard told us that he had to sort out things with some American archaeologists who were returning to the States that morning, but we could all meet for a pow-wow that afternoon. Forbes thought that to be acceptable as the Shangilla were expected to arrive, and he wanted to have a chat with them. In what language, I wondered, as Bob Campbell was the only person around that understood their dialect.

It was a little before noon, that the first sighting of the Shangilla was reported. David and I emerged from the equipment tent, and followed the gaze of everyone else along the shoreline. About a quarter of a mile away we could see three or four groups of men walking at a steady pace by the side of the lake.

'There looks to be more than fifteen of them,' said Bob, who had binoculars trained on them.

John Hemmingway thought there was double that number.

For me, the closer they came, the more beautiful they looked. Each one of them was only wearing a piece of sun-bleached sacking around their loins, like a knee-length skirt. Most of them carried a spear, and a few had machetes or knives strapped to their waists. They were all lean and perfectly muscled. A lot of them had elaborate coloured mud hairdos, and carried carved wooden neck supports to protect the hair when they slept. We were later told that the more complex patterns could take up to two or three days to complete. Their skins were almost pure black and shone like satin in the midday sun.

Striking as they were to look at, when they were twenty to thirty yards away, our gaze fell to what was hanging around their necks.

'Can you see any – thingies?' asked David.

'I can see some withered items on two of them,' I said.

'Are they – thingies?' urged David.

'One of them certainly could be, if you look closely,' I replied.

'I don't want to! You're the one with the medical kit.'

I wasn't sure what the medical kit had to do with this particular situation, as any surgery at this stage appeared to be futile.

'There's far too many of them,' said Forbes. 'I thought we asked for a dozen or so.'

'We did' said Bob, 'but to them, this is a dozen – or so.'

Bob spoke to them in a totally unknown dialect, which even John Hemmingway didn't follow, and he spoke fluent Swahili.

The amazing response of the tribesmen was to talk quietly among themselves for about five minutes. Two-thirds of them simply turned, and started the 70-mile walk back to their territory at the north of the lake. We were left with fourteen or fifteen Shangilla to represent life on earth at the beginning of time.

All appeared to be satisfactory, especially – as David pointed out – the men with the unfortunate doodads around their necks were in the group heading back home.

After the summit meeting with Richard Leakey in the afternoon, Martin, David, and myself were sitting in camping chairs on a sand spit some 30 metres from the camp. Drinking fruit juice, and watching the enormous crimson African sun going down behind the mountains on the opposite side of the lake, is a memory forever. We were totally engrossed in this sight when David pointed to a huge pink cloud travelling down the lake. It appeared to be only 20 or 30 feet above the water, and about a mile away. As it got closer, the cloud seemed to be travelling on wings, lots of wings. We didn't say anything, we sat in total silence as about 2,000 flamingos flew from somewhere in the north to somewhere else.

'That's the 5:45 p.m. flight to Lake Baringo,' said Liam, noticing our stupefaction, 'You'll see them most nights in July and August.' The remarkable thing is that we did see this totally amazing sight most nights, but by the second week, thousands of pink flamingos had become commonplace, and was simply the 5:45 to Baringo.

What kind of people are we?

The Kamba men looking after us were superb cooks, and the evening meals unusual, but always delicious. It was that evening Liam chose to terrify us by taking a powerful torch with a long beam of light. He slowly panned the torch along the black water of the lake and by looking down the beam of light; hundreds of eyes could be seen looking back at us.

'Crocodiles,' said Liam, 'hundreds of crocodiles.'

'But you let us go in the lake for a swim,' said David, 'and you said it was quite safe!'

'It is, during the daytime,' replied our trusted white hunter, 'but not at night.'

We reminisced on the luxurious feeling the lake water has on your skin. That afternoon we had all ventured into the lake as we had been told it was 'safe' – not a mention of crocodiles. The alkaline water felt like someone gently stroking your skin with the finest soft velvet. At 3:30 p.m. the water was tepid and had the hypnotic effect of persuading you to stay there forever.

I'm not sure if I should mention this, as some could interpret it as a kind of voyeurism, and now having said that, voyeurism is the first thing that will come into your mind. Of course, if I don't follow this line of thought, voyeurism will not be apparent.

It has to be appreciated that until this trip to Africa, I had only seen David fully clothed. That afternoon changed everything. David left the tent he was sharing with Martin in what I can only describe as designer, cut-away, Speedo swimming trunks.

The Kamba people stopped making tea. Forbes mentioned something about 'splendid seat on a horse.' Martin was already in the water and wallowing. John Hemmingway looked and muttered 'when you Limeys get it right, you get it right.' And I thought, How did David get his body into that remarkable condition? He resembled a compact edition of a Greek statue. And how does anyone get thighs to glow like that? And he still hadn't reached the water.

I thought I'd have to venture. The sooner I'm in the water no one will notice. I heaved my shape, which has been described as one with comfortable contours, into what had been adequate swimming trunks twelve years earlier, and made a sort of hurried lumber into the lake – it was simply wonderful.

After the meal, the three of us were sitting on our favourite sand spit. The gentle breeze was warm, and we could see lightning in the sky hundreds of miles to the south in the direction of Nairobi. Martin pointed out a couple of satellites tracking across the night sky. We noticed how clear the sky was, there was no light pollution for hundreds of miles, and the stars felt almost within reach. As we gazed into the sky I asked them if they had noticed the huge white cloud above us. David said he was just about to say the same; it was the brightest cloud he had ever seen in the night sky.

He had also noticed that the cloud was in the same place and had the same shape on the previous night. As we pointed the phenomenon out to Bob Campbell; he just mentioned that it could be the Milky Way. We felt he had to be right, as he went on to say that if you place a few hundred million, million stars in the sky at night, it could take on the appearance of being a bright cloud. David agreed, and mentioned he was about to say the same.

I'm not sure whether it was my sleeping habits or snoring, but Forbes had decided one night with me was enough, and had already made arrangements with Richard Leakey and his wife Maeve to have a room at their permanent camp.

At five o'clock next morning Forbes stuck his head through

my tent flap, and reminded me again that 'Africa Screams'. He then left and thoughtfully returned with a cup of tea.

After breakfast we were going over the plans for the day, when someone came running from the Leakey camp shouting 'They have a mandible! They actually have a mandible!'

'A mandible?' said Forbes, looking at John Hemmingway.

'Wow!' said Hemmingway, 'a mandible – that's great!'

Bob Campbell then turned up and told us the news: 'They have a mandible.'

'It's awfully exciting,' enthused Forbes, 'just imagine – a mandible.'

David was in the equipment tent doing 'camera things' and probably glowing a little. He had missed all the excitement; so I felt it was a matter of some urgency to get the news to him.

'They have a mandible,' I said trying to muster some excitement in my voice, which doesn't come easy to a Yorkshireman at 6:30 a.m.

'A what?' asked David.

'A mandible,' I said clearly, with a gesture of one who knows.

'What have they got?' he said.

The gesture of one who knows went limp, as I realised I didn't know of what I was the bearer.

'I think its some kind of a jawbone,' I mumbled.

Just then Martin came into the tent and said to David, 'Leakey's team have a mandible.'

'I know,' said David showing all his teeth, 'he just told me, but he doesn't know what it is.'

'It's a jawbone,' said Martin without a flourish. 'As soon as Leakey gets back we are going to fly out to the site and film it.'

'Does it do anything?' I asked.

'Its three-million-years-old – it doesn't do a lot,' said Martin with a grin.

We were getting to know each other pretty well. It felt good!

This particular Leakey site was managed by about six American archaeologists/ palaeontologists/ biologists, and about twenty Kenyan workers from the main camp. The buzz of excitement was pretty high, and the first thing Richard said to us on arrival was, 'Has anyone told you that we have a mandible?'

Forbes explained that the news had reached our camp, and then went into a huddle with the academics and Richard to arrange the best method of filming a jawbone which probably hadn't moved for three million years.

David and I sorted the gear out, and chatted to some of the second division academics who hadn't been included in the huddle.

It was decided that Richard would talk about the jawbone, whilst kneeling by it. He would then talk to the Kenyan who discovered it. Whether Richard should smoke his pipe throughout the talk appeared to be of some concern. Richard thought it would lend character. Forbes felt it could prove difficult in the edit, depending on which way the wind was blowing the smoke, left to right or right to left. John Hemmingway said, 'Heavens to Betsy – it's only a pipe! Let's shoot some film.'

Bob Campbell smiled and said quietly, 'There's no hurry, the mandible isn't going anywhere.'

David and I just looked at each other, and didn't smile (until much later).

The compromise was to film Richard with his pipe, but not alight, hence no smoke right to left or left to right, and Richard had his pipe lending character. There's not a lot you can do on camera with an unlit pipe-accompanied palaeontologist, kneeling by a three-million-year-old mandible which wasn't moving very much.

Later in the week a decision was made to film the Shangilla sharing food. Part of Richard's theory was that early man was a food sharer and that was how they survived. All well and good, now we needed a dead animal to be shared by our local representatives of early man – the Shangilla.

'No problem,' said Liam, 'I have a permit to kill ten oryx or ten topi, as needed.'

Forbes had been told that early man, not having any Swiss Army knives, would have used flint pieces to cut the animal hide. The cutting was also easier to if the animal had been freshly killed.

'No problem,' said Liam, 'I'll be with you on the shoot for

protection against lion attack so I can pick off an animal, and you can get to work.'

Forbes thought this to be a jolly good idea, so we set off with ten of our 'early men' in search of a good location.

Martin thought that as almost everything looked like a lunar landscape, wouldn't it be better to drive towards the herd of topi half a mile away and shoot one of them. It was agreed, this also was a jolly good idea.

A topi is about the size of a small horse, and usually moves around slowly in large herds eating the long grass. The herd in front of us today was estimated by Bob Campbell to number around two thousand. Most of these were eating the grass and therefore stationary, and an easy target. The Shangilla were particularly patient and very quiet. It dawned on us later that they can't have had the remotest idea what was happening – after all, we were pretty much making it up as we went along.

Liam was kneeling on one knee with an impressive looking rifle at his shoulder. At that moment we all felt a common bond of security as Liam adopted the 'white hunter' position, and took aim at a stationary topi fifty metres away.

Our eyes were fixed on the topi, when we heard the bang. A few topi moved away and continued to eat grass.

'I'll adjust the sights,' said Liam. 'That'll fix it.'

Liam adopted the position once more, another loud bang, and the topi moved and went on eating. Three attempts later, a topi finally dropped. Thankfully, it was a straight kill and not a serious wound.

It was crossing my mind right there and then that it had taken Liam five shots to kill a stationary animal, the size of a horse, eating grass, and only fifty yards away. He was our security against lion attack, and lions don't stand around eating grass, they move pretty quickly towards you when you happen to be on the lunch menu.

David muttered to me, 'It took him five shots, what chance have we got if it's a croc or a lion?'

'I know,' I whispered, not wishing to advertise our white hunter's lack of marksmanship.

The Shangilla had been given some previously prepared flint

stones with razor-sharp edges to cut into the animal. They were eager to get at it, as they had been promised a share of the spoils before the vultures arrived.

The animal was turned over to hide the bullet hole: after all, we don't want any of that sort of stuff on camera, this programme goes out on American TV when people are eating their evening meal. Three Shangilla were selected to cut open the corpse, and we began to film the sequence. After a minute of vigorous cutting action with a piece of flint, it became quite obvious that it wasn't going to penetrate the hide. Another bit of flint was tried with the same result.

'Do you have a Stanley knife in your tool kit?' asked Forbes.
I nodded.
'Could you get it, please?' said Forbes.
I nodded again.

Bob Campbell explained to the Shangilla what was about to happen, and they looked pretty pleased at the thought of having rump steak for supper. Bob made a short incision into the shoulder of the topi with the Stanley knife, we turned the camera and sound on, and the Shangilla started to carve large pieces of meat from the animal with the flint.

'Can you get them to keep the blood to a minimum?' asked John Hemmingway. 'Meal-time transmission, you know.'

'It's looking great,' said Martin, as the shiny black skins of the Shangilla turned blood red.

We did get a good sequence, and Richard told us, 'That's more or less how early man would have gathered their food' – conveniently forgetting to mention the Stanley knife.

As we drove away from the remains of the carcass, David pointed to four or five vultures which had already landed and were clawing at the animal, and in the sky at least a dozen more were gliding in to the kill, and this was from a clear blue sky with not a vulture in sight when we began the sequence.

One evening towards the end of the second week, we were sitting on the sand spit, drinking our bitter lemons and assorted juices, and mulling over the odd million or so years we had been recently introduced to, when Martin noticed two satellites tracking across the sky. Whether these were the same pair we had previously seen, who could tell, but we were debating how far away they were when five of the Shangilla pushed a crude boat into the lake, which had been carved from a tree. David mentioned he had heard they were going to catch a crocodile for their supper, as we hadn't provided any topi burgers recently.

Forbes called to us that dinner was ready and the Kamba had prepared a surprise for us. The meal was, as usual, very tasty, but we hadn't spotted any surprise.

Liam was entertaining us with some hilarious stories of a 'white hunter' when there was the most almighty turmoil, shouting and thrashing in the lake.

Three of the Shangilla were in the water, and in the light of our torches we could make out two of them wrestling with a crocodile, while the two in the boat were ramming spears into its head. To us the crocodile appeared to be more alive than dead, and the men in the water seemed to be in severe peril.

Shortly, a few others arrived to assist in the capture. Somehow they managed to get a rope around the croc's head and someone had jammed a machete into its mouth to stop it closing. They got another rope around it and began to drag it out of the lake. Once on the shore, they discovered they had a very upset crocodile which wasn't taking kindly to this kind of treatment.

Forbes chose this moment to lean over to me and say quietly, 'How unlike the home life of our own dear Queen!'

Amazingly, they managed to kill the croc, and even more amazingly, only one of the Shangilla had been hurt by its thrashing tail.

We had just been served a delicious meal by the Kamba people, and then watched eight or nine men armed with a few spears and a machete risk their lives to feed themselves and their friends. We were still bewildered by what we had just witnessed when the dessert arrived.

Benson was carrying a silver tray with two lit candles either side of a large glass bowl, and in the bowl was a decorated sherry trifle. The silver tray was placed on the table, and we all applauded Benson and his team; it was a fine looking trifle. Over Benson's shoulder we could see our 'early men' dragging the recently deceased croc to its final resting place at their camp. I felt the applause was really more for them.

It was at that point a form of cognitive dissonance came to rest on us.

Martin was shaking his head thoughtfully and asked, 'How do you relate a croc fighting for its life, and those men fighting for their lives, with the billions of dollars spent on two tracking satellites, and the incongruity of us being served sherry trifle by a man called Benson, who was named after a cigarette? Added to that, how do you explain the satellites to the Shangilla, who didn't understand their own reflection in the wing mirror on a Land Rover?'

On August 9th we flew up to one of the American sites to film some new discoveries and to interview a US archaeologist who had some interesting theories on Richard's dating methods. The plane touched down on a dirt strip 200 yards from the site, and was greeted by happy, cheering Americans who were drinking champagne. We naturally thought, as it was only 7:30 a.m., they must have discovered a real 'Godzilla' of a skull, at least four or five million years old.

We got off the plane to have female and male archaeologists flinging their arms around us, and showering us with champagne.

'Isn't it absolutely ace fantastic? Nixon's resigned!'

'They will probably impeach him,' said a learned-looking man who didn't smoke a pipe.

'We heard it on the radio this morning, and I don't know where the champagne came from, but it is cold, do you want some?'

So we did.

We didn't film much for the next few hours, but shared the total joy with the American academics.

Not long after the Nixon news broke, Forbes decided to shoot a couple of sequences on the two major finds made by the Leakey team. This was a complete skull of an Australopithecus found in a dried up riverbed by Richard and his then girlfriend Maeve. The skull was thought to be three-million-years-old. The other find was a fragmented skull discovered by Bernard Ngeneo, one of Richard's key workmen, but it was Maeve who assembled the skull from the dozens of pieces found by Bernard. He also smokes a pipe, but doesn't wear a beret.

'How Unlike the Home Life of Our Own Dear Queen'

The assembled skull was about the size of a human head and was called '1470'. I don't think anybody explained why it was called 1470, but no matter, when it was found in 1972 it was dated as being three-million-years-old.

Now this news had grabbed scientists by the lapels worldwide, thoroughly shaking them. Archaeologists applauded, said 'Well done' and got excited. Palaeontologists had their academic noses tweaked and felt uncomfortable. Just how uncomfortable, I had never realised until later in the shoot.

During this time, it was felt by the majority of those who mattered that Richard was an all round 'good egg'.

Unfortunately, some learned scholar had pointed out to the press that there was some confusion in the scientific world, which understood 1470 to have descended from australopithecines, and therefore could not be older than that from which they had descended.

It is said among those who know about these things, that many pipes were smoked, and numerous huddles encountered before a spanking new date was arrived at for a skull named 1470. It was now one and a half-million-years-old and everybody was happy again.

Well, almost everybody.

Forbes was in top form in a dried-up riverbed with Richard and Maeve, along with the very skull they had discovered and were about to discover all over again for the camera. He felt it was time to introduce a bit of drama into the programme, and by jingo he was going to do it. John Hemmingway had no objections, so a huddle was formed and a carefully detailed script was prepared for Richard and Maeve.

Meanwhile, the skull had been placed in a specially dug hole in the riverbed, with only its cranium showing, ready to be rediscovered.

Both Richard and Maeve were wearing radio microphones so Martin could shoot the sequence as widely as he wished. The idea being that Richard and Maeve would walk down the riverbed, spot the Australopithecus and launch into their rehearsed dialogue.

As we were into drama, Forbes felt we could rehearse the

dialogue – providing Richard and Maeve didn't walk down the riverbed leaving the telltale evidence of footprints in the sand.

'Forget it,' said Richard, who had been stripped of his pipe, but not his beret. 'We'll do it for real, after all there's not much dialogue.' As it turned out Richard was right, there certainly wasn't much dialogue.

Forbes was on a high. 'Let's shoot it!' he cried, and Martin agreed. 'Let's shoot it.'

'Turn over!' called Forbes.

Camera and sound turned over.

'Mark it,' said Martin.

David called the number, and snapped the clapperboard.

Gosh – we were good!

'Action!' shouted Forbes with directorial authority.

Richard and Maeve adopted a thoughtful expression and walked down the riverbed in peaceful meditation, suddenly Maeve looked in the direction of the half-buried skull and immediately exclaimed to Richard, 'Oh, look Richard, it's an Australopithecus!'

Richard paused and looked even more thoughtful. 'You're right,' he said positively, 'It *is* an Australopithecus.'

Pause.

'Cut!' called Forbes, with even more authority, and sliced himself across the throat with his hand.

That was the dialogue? That was the drama?

I looked at David, who bit his bottom lip, but fortunately didn't laugh. David looked at Martin, who then looked at me, and fortunately nobody laughed.

'I thought that went rather well,' said Forbes with an encouraging smile.

'So did I,' said Richard, warming to his newly acquired thespian leanings.

'Concise and to the point,' said John Hemmingway. 'Easy to follow – Americans like that.'

'Well, then – that's splendid,' said somebody.

During the last week a small plane arrived with a fresh intake of palaeontologists, archaeologists and a zoologist. The new arrivals were from the UK and were to stay a few days to observe what had been discovered recently and to have a friendly chat with their colleagues from the USA. Perhaps 'friendly' is the wrong word, as I had yet to discover that these people are passionately and fiercely competitive, and are quite likely to lop off a million or two years here or there depending on their own theories.

They all had interesting, if varying, opinions on Richard's thesis, particularly on the 1470 skull. Academics are often entertaining, especially if they have a sense of humour, and this particular coterie didn't disappoint.

I was surprised to find two of them showing no sense of disbelief when they became aware of my creationist thoughts, although one of them did point out that in the entire workforce at Rudolf, I was probably the only creationist around, and at best considered some kind of alien.

I smiled and agreed, 'That does appear to be the case.'

One evening, I was sitting with two of the visitors and John Hemmingway, when one of them asked me, what was the problem I had with the Big Bang and Darwin? This surprised me, as people are not usually that direct.

I attempted to explain that the Big Bang had never rung true for me ever since I left school in 1953, as explosions leave only total chaos. One only has to talk to the survivors of Hiroshima and Nagasaki to realise the absolute devastation caused by those two big bangs, and the Big Bang science puts on offer is infinitely greater than that of Hiroshima.

I thought this could be a good time to pose the idea of the Big Bang 'theory' being unable to be a theory. I understood that scientifically a theory was only accepted as a theory after it had been tested hundreds and hundreds of times, in varying situations and locations. The Big Bang, by its very definition, could never have been tested as it would only have happened once, and according to the world of science and evolution, the scientists who would have done the testing did not evolve until over 15 billion years after the alleged Big Bang.

'Should it possibly be called the Big Bang Idea?' I ventured.

'There are many scientists who would share your view,' said one of the visitors.

I thought I might have a creationist colleague on my left, lurking under his professorial bearing.

'How about Darwin?' asked the other one.

I told him I shared the same doubts that Darwin himself shared about his so-called 'theory of evolution.'

I'd listened to a doctor talk about the complexity of the human eye and its ability to differentiate between dark and light, plus the thousands of colours it observes and separates. This medical reasoning persuades me that the eye could not have evolved. One eye consultant reasoned in a lecture that the human eye only worked correctly if it was 100% perfect. Should it be only 50% or 70% complete, as it would have to have been during some point in 'evolution', the owners of these partially developed eyes would simply have been blind, and therefore have fallen from the so-called evolutionary chain in which the owner was involved.

Another mystery, which seemed to cause Darwin great trouble, was that of blood clotting. Fortunately we have far more scientific evidence today than Darwin, but the evidence only supports the mystery of blood clotting, and demonstrates clearly how it could not have evolved. Apparently when the skin is cut, a sticky protein is released in a controlled manner, which stops the loss of blood, protects against germs and helps to form a protective scab. This protein, though, is a deadly toxin when left uncontrolled, and would cause death quickly if left floating around your body. This protein is apparently only kicked into action when the skin is cut or broken. It seems to me that this is one of the biggest problems an evolutionist has to figure out.

Darwin couldn't figure it out, and actually described the whole blood-clotting process as an inexplicably complex system, and also admitted that it was one of the things that could wreck his whole idea.

'Both your reasons are adequate grounds for doubting evolution, but wouldn't you agree that only a step of faith in a Divine Creator is all that is needed?' asked the friendly professor.

I nodded and replied, 'It appears that much more faith is required to believe in evolution, and the Big Bang, than is needed to believe in God.'

John Hemmingway looked a little perplexed and said, 'I'm turning in, goodnight and thank you.'

The last days we spent at Lake Rudolf had the feel of dreaming. Were we about to wake up and find ourselves back in London?

It hadn't been a dream. There were the Shangilla catching tilapia for their supper. Pink flamingos at 5:45 p.m. – satellites – the Milky Way – an Australopithecus – vast herds of topi, zebra and oryx – the occasional lions – a 'white hunter' – great stories, intrepid, but a lousy shot – more palaeontologists than would fit in a Mini – Nixon resigned – Benson and his tea – David's glowing thighs, which were now dark Bourneville – crocodiles at night – Richard Leakey and his pipe, give or take a million years – the charming Forbes… and *Africa still screamed*.

I woke up at 5 a.m. on the last morning only to find David up before me, but then this had been par for the course over the last six weeks. We both watched the Shangilla, who were watching us watching them. They were standing still, not speaking, just looking.

'Do you think anybody has told them we are leaving today?' asked David.

'Well, Bob's the only one who can speak to them and I haven't seen him about yet,' I replied.

'Do you think they are armed?' said David.

'They usually are,' I said.

'That's not what I wanted to hear – go away.'

The Kamba men were packing up the camp and loading the trucks. The site was beginning to look a little barren when two light aircraft landed on the strip to fly us back to Nairobi.

Bob came over and told us the Shangilla were about to leave. They made some gestures, which we hoped meant castration was not at the forefront of their minds, but 'Farewell' and 'Goodbye' was. The small group just turned and walked away from us on the 70-mile trek to the north of Lake Rudolf. It was all very matter of fact, no one could accuse them of 'standing upon their going'.

From 200 feet up Lake Rudolf did have the appearance of a jade sea, and glistened in the sunlight. The plane banked gently and Richard Leakey's permanent camp on the headland could be seen receding slowly into the haze.

Nairobi felt very crowded after the space of Lake Rudolf, but this was shopping time. We had family and friends back home

'How Unlike the Home Life of Our Own Dear Queen'

who were expecting African goodies on our return, so shopping was imminent. We had three days to unwind, one of them taken up filming at the Nairobi Museum with Richard, and possibly his pipe. The next day to pack the gear, and the final day to attend the official function at the New Stanley Hotel, which included dinner.

Martin had previously spent time with David in Iran and other distant places, and had already advised me that when David goes shopping its best not to go with him, or even to ask any questions.

On the last day when David said he was going shopping, I heeded Martin's advice and waved to him as he was driven off in a taxi, apparently by a man called Marlborough. I made a note to ask David if his driver was in any way related to Benson.

I headed for downtown Nairobi and bought a collection of things which looked very African, if a little frightening, and knew these would do for my children, who weren't very old it the time but would grow to like them.

When I got back to the Norfolk Hotel, where we were staying, there was a message from David asking me to join him for tea in the hotel lounge at four o'clock. This seemed like a nice idea, we could then go on to the function at the New Stanley.

Forbes had advised us to turn up clean and wearing smart, tidy clothing, possibly not jeans. Smart, tidy was the forerunner to smart casual, which in 1974 hadn't been thought of. We had been offered ties by a gentleman of the Nairobi Club, who had told us that ties would be in evidence at the function, and he didn't wish us to feel out of place, don't you know. We thanked him for his concern and etiquette, but we were suitably catered for and embarrassment would not be to the fore.

I showered and tried to ease myself into some 1972 flares, which fortunately went on without the aid of Vaseline, and after applying more than a liberal amount of body deodorant I went down to the hotel lounge to find David.

The Norfolk Hotel was a part of old Nairobi, and although the Empire had left Kenya, this wonderful hotel still carried the atmosphere of Dr Livingstone and Stanley. As I entered the lounge I spotted David sitting comfortably in a large armchair. I looked towards him, made a friendly gesture and David smiled. I walked towards him unaware that he was still smiling a lot. When I sat down opposite him, David hissed through an even larger smile, 'Would I like some tea?'

I thought, Well, that's why I'm here. So I said, 'Yes please.'

I also thought, Something's odd.

David lifted his hand gracefully, and a lovely Kenyan waiter brought the tea to us. David hissed at him through a smile difficult to describe and said, 'Thank you, my good man.'

This wasn't like David, who had now turned to me and grinned. 'Shall I pour, sweetie?' he asked.

Well, he hadn't referred to me as 'sweetie' before, but I thought, 'sweetie' had better say 'yes'.

Smiling, David poured the tea, which was as usual delicious, and then continued to smile.

He then started to hiss and then to laugh. I hadn't said anything, and as far as I could see there was nothing around us to laugh at.

'Are you alright?' I asked.

'Oh you beautiful, wonderful inhothent!' he said.

He said 'inhothent', I thought.

'Would you like a thmoke? Hi have some...hin my room.' Grin, smile.

I knew at that point I needed help, and went to call Martin.

Fortunately, a smart, tidy Martin was down in a few minutes, and when he saw David with the expression on his face, he muttered something like 'Good grief, he's had a joint.'

'A joint?' I said.

'He's smoked some grass,' said Martin, 'and the stuff out here is pretty potent.'

David sat and smiled. He looked very happy with his mahogany tan and perfect, super white teeth.

'What time are we due at the New Stanley?' asked Martin.

'Six o'clock,' I replied.

'We'll walk him there, that'll burn some off.' Martin said.

'How much will it burn off?' I asked him.

'Not a lot,' he said.

David smiled a most beautiful smile, stood to attention, saluted a picture of 'the Queen' and under another muted smile

'How Unlike the Home Life of Our Own Dear Queen'

muttered 'Charming Lady.'
Oh 'eck, I thought.

The walk from the Norfolk Hotel to the New Stanley lasted about half an hour, but this did little to abate David's permanent smile, accompanied by the slight hiss.

The colonial-looking room allocated for the do was set out with military precision. Tables had been lined up in strict 'U' formation, with place names set rigidly, as those in the know jolly well knew it ought to be. Nothing had been left to chance; after all, film technicians were on the loose at this function, and two of them loose cannons from Yorkshire!

Martin and myself where not sitting next to David, but were within grabbing distance should anything unfortunate surface.

The meal was going well, with a plethora of 'white hunters' apparent wearing suitable safari outfits, as well as the 'worthy' of Nairobi.

Liam Linn was on the top table as appropriate, along with Forbes, John Hemmingway, Richard Leakey and Maeve, plus a few random colonials, as yet unknown.

It was obvious to me that at a gathering such as this, after the food, speeches would be par for the course from the above-mentioned dignitaries.

Now this is all very well, if you don't have a time bomb called David in the wings, waiting to explode.

David doesn't disappoint.

Forbes made a courteous, formal speech, which was very correct for the occasion, and we all clapped.

John Hemmingway made a similar speech – translated into American – which was also very correct for the occasion, and we all clapped again.

Richard Leakey was about a minute into his talk when David decided the room was too hot. Unfortunately, Martin and I were going through our 'engrossed with every word, Richard' routine, instead of keeping an eye on David. It only took him a few seconds to be out of his seat and to disappear behind a huge curtain in search of windows.

The curtain measured from floor to the ceiling, and appeared to be made from carpet material. Despite the weight of the fabric David was making good progress as he punched his way along the back.

Richard, all power to him, didn't flinch but carried on; after all, he was now in full flow.

Martin leant forward to me and said, 'Get him out, you're nearest.'

A few people close to us began to smile, and look round at the frantic bulge behind the curtain.

'Is he looking for the lavatory?' whispered the gentleman from the Nairobi Club who had offered us ties.

I shook my head. 'He's trying to find a window to open,' I said quietly.

'There aren't any windows on that wall; the curtain is only for decoration,' he said. 'I know because my company supplied the curtain.'

The blows from behind the curtain were becoming more violent.

Fortunately, Richard had said something humorous, and the laughter masked the sound of the blows to the curtain.

By now David had worked his way to the far end of the curtain, only to discover a shortage of windows on his side. He stuck his head out, and looked at faces staring at him that he had never seen in his life before, and his head shot behind the curtain again.

For the next couple of minutes the curtain didn't move. Martin and I didn't take our eyes off it.

Richard had now got to the main thrust of his speech and was winding down with thanks to Forbes, John and Survival TV Anglia.

The first clap of the applause for Richard's speech was like a starting pistol to David, who decided to make a dash for it along the back of the curtain.

He emerged at our end of the curtain stupefied by applause, and thinking it was for him bowed low in true thespian style, and sat down with a 'Garfield' grin stuck to his face.

Martin looked at me and I looked at Martin – and smiled.

'How Unlike the Home Life of Our Own Dear Queen'

On the flight home to London, David told me about the events leading up to the cup of tea at the Norfolk Hotel.

Apparently, any taxi driver will know where 'the action' is, and Marlborough true to his profession did not let David down.

Marlborough, who was named after Winston Churchill's school, had a father who admired Churchill to the point of calling his first son Winston, and his second son after the school. Marlborough drove David to meet another taxi driver who had cousins in the 'Smoke' business, and had a quantity of 'grass' for sale. David was the customer with the cash.

When David got back to the hotel he rolled a joint just to check the quality, and discovered it to be only the best. He was pleased with his purchase, but that was all he remembered for some time.

I did explain to him about his Oscar-winning performance from our side of the curtain with his exit, and Olivier-style bow, which seemed to please him and mirrored his thespian teenage years. I'll never know how much he did remember.

Three incredibly suntanned film technicians mused over the real adventure they had experienced during the last six weeks, and decided each had undergone a change. It had drawn us closer together, and we now knew for certain that Africa truly does scream.

Christmas in Lesotho

The Children's Film Foundation had booked Martin, David and myself to work on a children's feature film during December and January 1975. The location was Lesotho, a small mountainous landlocked country inside South Africa, which used to be part of the British Empire. As this was a feature film I had the luxury of having a boom swinger to assist me and good fortune gave me Peter Glossop – a sound man; very easy to be with and professional to a T.

In early December David, Peter and I left London on what turned out to be a most peculiar route to Johannesburg – Martin had flown ahead of us two weeks earlier, with the director Tim King, to complete a recce of Mantsonyane, a small town in the mountains where the film would be shot. The British Airways flight to Paris was par for the course, and the Air France flight to Nice was uneventful. At Nice we boarded a plane of unknown origin and headed for West Africa.

The itinerary told us that the first stop in Africa would be Libreville in Gabon, where we expected to arrive at around 4 a.m. As we had been travelling for some twelve hours already and it was now midnight, Peter and I dozed off. David, who had apparently partied in his usual style the previous evening with much hospitality, tried to sleep; but his digestive system had other ideas.

As we approached Libreville, we were awakened by the captain telling us, over a scratchy intercom, that it would be a bumpy landing as a tropical rainstorm was coming down like stair rods, the runway was flooded, humidity a hundred per cent, and the temperature 38°. I looked out of the window, and in the beam of the landing lights I could see that the captain was telling the absolute truth, the rain was indeed coming down like stair rods with only a few millimetres between each rod – visibility was practically nil. Well, what the heck, I thought, these pilots are jungle trained; they know what they are doing. I should have mentioned that we were sitting about four rows from the rear of the plane with a row of three toilets across the back. The captain came on the intercom again and asked us to make sure we were strapped in firmly as we would be landing in about a minute. I was busy making sure that I was firmly strapped in when the plane hit the runway, testing the hydraulics to the full. We were then airborne again for a moment before landing very firmly, and it was at this point that the toilet door just behind burst open and David travelled past me down the aisle with his trousers round his ankles, trying to brake himself by grabbing the seats. David came to a standstill a few rows in front and, with incredible skill, quickly slid his trousers over his hips, turned, grinned, and walked back to the toilet acknowledging the smiles and laughter of the passengers in the back few rows. When the plane had stopped, David came back, sat next to me, and said with a grin, 'I do not believe I just did that.'

We were in Africa.

After a journey of twenty-six hours, the arrival at Jan Smuts Airport in Johannesburg was a wonderful relief. Jo'burg was to be home for the next three days while we picked up a vehicle and other items necessary for the filming.

On our way to the city by taxi, the white South African driver was silent for the entire 30-minute journey, except for telling us, 'Did you know, it is a criminal offence for white men to have sexual intercourse with black women in South Africa?' This was all he said. To us it seemed obvious, that he knew, from all the metal cases we had loaded into the two taxis following us, we must be on drugs, or had a severe drink problem, probably smoked pot and were total reprobates.

Welcome to South Africa!

The Chevrolet truck was a monster, brand new with only 53 miles on the clock. Stuck to the dashboard was a note advising us not to drive faster than 40 mph. This was not good news, as the drive across the Transvaal to Lesotho was the best part of 300 miles and we had already had some difficulty steering our way around the finer points of apartheid. Our diplomacy was being stretched. Come to think of it, are there any finer points to apartheid?

Christmas in Lesotho

We spent three interesting days meeting various people in Johannesburg who were to help us collect the items we required for the journey, and the rest of the time attempting to come to terms with the Chevrolet gearbox. None of us had come across a gearbox quite like it, and we each had a different theory as to why the vehicle appeared to need seven gears, with optional four-wheel drive in forward and reverse (or it could have been the other way round).

If you've travelled with David a lot, you soon get used to his habit of disappearing suddenly. It's not that he no longer wishes to be in your company, rather more that he has vital business to attend to. This can come in many forms, but usually a deal has been struck somewhere in the city, and we all benefit from the venture. How he knows who to contact in a city he has never been to before I could never discover, but on this occasion I know we ended up getting more rand to the pound or to the US dollar than we did at the bank or the hotel. There was, however, a further deal, which had been set up for the following day, as we left Johannesburg for Lesotho.

David at that time had two immaculate Olympus camera bodies with an assortment of lenses one could only covet. As so often happened in David's life, Olympus would bring out a new lens, which any photographer worth their tripod would have to have. Such was the case in Johannesburg; David had found a camera shop, which not only had the new lens (still unavailable in the UK) but at least a hundred pounds less than the provisional price back in Blighty. A chance like this could not be missed, and of course we all understood it would only take us a couple of streets out of our way.

I had been elected to drive the first leg of the journey, and so on the morning of departure the monster truck moved through the city in whatever gear I could find to propel it forward. David, for some unclear reason, with a look on his face I had seen before, suggested it would be better if Peter and I stayed in the vehicle, and park it just around the corner – out of sight of the shop. Now on these occasions I never argue with David; if he says 'round the corner', then round the corner it is. Peter, who hadn't travelled with David before, asked me what, was going on. I assured him all

Christmas in Lesotho

was fine, David was only thinking about us. I realised, as I said this, it didn't make much sense, and Peter certainly knew it didn't make any sense at all.

We sat in the truck watching the good people of Johannesburg pass by, and the people of Johannesburg looked at the monster truck and wondered why such a vehicle should be parked outside a ladies' hat shop with assorted lingerie on the first floor.

The passenger side door flew open and a parcel was thrown in which landed by Peter's feet – this was followed very quickly by David who threw himself in and also landed at Peter's feet shouting, '*Drive, drive, drive!*'

In that state of panic, I knew, as the oldest one present, it was my responsibility to maintain calm and offer assurance, so I said, 'Hang on, I'll find a gear.'

'Just *drive!*' shouted David 'They're coming!'

Now I have to say at this point, that was the first I had heard about any extras being involved, but it did assist me in finding a gear. Unfortunately, I managed to find the low register of the four-wheel drive, and we made a lethargic getaway at all of 4 mph flat out, with David urging me to find a better one. I remember making a mental note at the time – when doing my next bank job not to use a Chevy truck as a getaway vehicle.

We finally left the city boundary at a handsome speed of 25 mph with the three of us, now sitting on the front bench seat, trying our best not to look at one another. I could hear muted noises coming from David, which usually means he's pleased with the deal and his latest acquisition. About five miles outside Johannesburg, I pulled the truck into a lay-by so we could look at the contents of the parcel still at Peter's feet.

David picked up the very new Olympus box and started to unwrap his trophy, at the same time extolling the virtues of this new lens over any others on the market. He was now pulling at the protective wrapping quite excitedly to reveal the treasured lens, but instead produced half a house brick.

David had just spent £120 on half a house brick.

We spent a lot of time laughing on that journey, and all power to David he was laughing as much as we were.

As it turned out, the journey across the Transvaal was one of the most spectacular and beautiful I have ever taken. Many shades of green, hills and mountains in the distance, a warm-to-hot climate and little humidity; its hardly surprising that the settlers were happy with their lot, having arrived at what must have appeared to many as Eden. The Chevrolet travelling at a sedate 40 mph and with its high wheelbase gave us the perfect vantage point to take in the vast and stunning scenery.

It was about 8 p.m. when we crossed the border post from the Orange Free State into Lesotho. Fortunately the capital, Maseru, is not far from the border, and in twenty minutes we were parking the monster truck in the forecourt of our hotel. We were congratulating ourselves on the driving and the journey when I noticed a black face smiling at us by the vehicle. I wound the window down and was about to ask him if it was okay to leave the truck parked here overnight, when he said to us with an even broader grin, 'My name is Michael – I'm a pimp. Do you want nice black girl?'

I explained that we had just driven from Johannesburg and all we wanted was to check in to the hotel and unload some of our cases. And by the way, isn't your offer of nice black girl a "criminal offence"?' I added.

'Not in Lesotho,' he said, smiled again and as he walked away called, 'In Lesotho – black girl okay.'

In the morning we met up with Martin, Tim and some of the children who were to take part in the film. Tim or someone from the University in Maseru told us not, under any circumstances, to mention Queen Victoria. Lesotho was a happy member of the British Empire until the early 1950s when it was decided to give them their independence. This did not go down well with the Basuto people, who argued that the British government had broken the agreement made between Queen Victoria and their country, and please could we take them back.

We set off quite early on our journey from Maseru to Mantsonyane as Tim had warned us that although it was only about 60 miles, the roads were mountainous, rocky, and in some cases non-existent. In December, Lesotho has wonderful clear sunny mornings, but about midday it darkens and the deluge takes over. Not only had some of the roads disappeared, but also when they reappeared in the sunshine on the following morning, they were not the same shape you had driven on the previous day.

Eight hours later we arrived at Mantsonyane, a small town almost 10,000 ft up on the western side of the Drakensberg Mountains. I suppose the reason it qualified as a town could have been that it had a hospital, a school, a church, and a hazardous airstrip. We found it rather disconcerting that a South African called Dr DeAth was the hospital administrator. The locals were delighted to see us and gave us a great welcome. It appeared that many of the local men got around on horseback, and wore very strange mixtures of military uniforms. The social status of a man in Mantsoyane seemed to be measured by the number of lavatory chains he wore on his uniform; we knew they were lavatory chains because they still had the pull handles attached. The 'hotel' we were shown to by our hosts was a breeze-block collection of single rooms joined together by a common corridor. Each of us had a room, no more than 10 ft by 6 ft, with a wardrobe, a washbasin, and some kind of arrangement to supply running water – hot or cold wasn't a choice. At the far end of the breeze-block corridor was a bathroom, which was a little larger than our rooms, and two extremely small toilets adjacent to the bathroom. So this breeze-block bunker was to be home for the next seven weeks.

It was only a couple of days before we were involved in our first debate with some of the senior locals. The topic quite naturally was Queen Victoria and how could the British renege on a deal made with a British Queen. To these gentlemen of Mantsonyane we must have incredible clout, as we had all these silver cases with expensive looking things inside, and on top of that, had flown from London (which is on the other side of the world) to South Africa, and spend seven weeks living with them in a hotel which had been built specially for us only a few weeks before. We had to be gentlemen of some substance. One of them leant forward and told us, in a most discreet manner, that actually – we probably didn't know this – but we were the first people ever to stay in the hotel.

David, who was probably the cleanest of the crew members,

Christmas in Lesotho

decided he would like to try out the rather spacious bathroom. He had only been gone a couple of minutes when he came to my room very unwashed. 'Come and have a look at this – you will never believe it,' he said. We both went down to the bathroom and as we got closer I could hear the sounds of splashing water. 'There's someone using it,' I said. David smiled, shook his head in disbelief at my astute observation and said, 'You are absolutely right, someone is using the bathroom… and also something.' A man was washing his horse in the bathroom. After all, why shouldn't a man wash his horse in a perfectly built room with a concrete floor, and plenty of running water pumped from the stream outside from which he had always washed his horse? It was the same stream and the same water. We both agreed the horse did appear to be quite at home. However, the incident did help to forge feelings in me that in the future, whenever booking into a hotel anywhere in the world, I would be happy as long as I didn't have to share the bathroom with a horse.

With all this washing of horses, it had been noticed that the toilet rolls in the adjacent latrines were pretty wet, as they were resting on the floor. We were not sure whether the rolls were simply wet from the amount of water in the area, or whether it was a mixture of other equine fluids. The real problem wasn't the washing of horses, but the lack of toilet roll holders in the toilets. We decided to meet the situation head-on. I believe it was Martin who sketched a simple but effective drawing of a perfectly competent toilet-roll holder made from pieces of wood from a box and a broom handle. Martin indicated that when made the roll would fit on to the cut-down broom handle and the whole device could be fitted to the inside of the door, thus keeping the roll dry. This all seemed to be understood and the following day we left the sketch and instructions with the hotel owner, we went off to do another day's filming.

In the late afternoon we returned to the hotel to be greeted by an excited owner, who took some of us to see the deluxe improvements in the 'usual offices'. He or somebody had most certainly constructed a most magnificent toilet-roll holder and fitted it firmly to the inside of the door, about three feet off the floor. He was keen to point out any water from future horse play would not reach that height. We all agreed it was a splendid toilet-roll holder, but it was rather large. Our error was quite obvious; we had assumed foolishly, that the size of a toilet-roll would automatically give you an obvious size for its corresponding holder, so we had not put any dimensions on our sketch. The construction was such that when visiting this very small room, it became impossible to close the door, except by grabbing the toilet roll holder and pulling it towards you. By now, you were sitting down on the pan, as the toilet roll was firmly in your chest pinning you to the back wall. It was impossible to reach forward and lock the door. Adjustments were made.

Martin had taken to greeting any Basuto at the outset of the day with 'How ya diddlin'?' and this had taken off in a big way. The young children had adopted Martin wholesale, and mimicked almost everything he said or did, even his walk.

After a couple of weeks, the children were greeting all of us with 'How ya diddlin'?' and we would reply, 'Fine' or 'okay'.

It was about this time that a teacher from their school came to see us, and asked, 'What is this "diddlin"' I hear the children saying all the time?'

Martin explained that it was just something Don Whillans, a Yorkshire mountaineer, had said on Mount Everest some years ago, when, not having been seen for three days at 26,000 feet, he turned up at base camp and to the amazement of his fellow climbers simply said, 'How ya diddlin'?'

The teacher said, 'As 95% of the children are using "diddlin"' on a regular daily basis, I will have to accept that it is now part of the English vocabulary in Lesotho.'

Christmas at 10,000 ft in Lesotho was different, and the Basuto people were determined that we should have a good time. Come the 25th, we were escorted to another breeze-block building less than a spit from our hotel where leaders from neighbouring villages had ridden in to give 'the new kids on the breeze block' a quick once-over. The rumour had obviously spread far, as some of these men had been riding for over a day or two to get there. The news of men with metal boxes, who could reunite the Basuto people with Queen Victoria's descendants on their return to

England, was certainly worth a couple of days in the saddle. The fact we had incredible clout was now out and could not be concealed any further.

Tim, our director, who naturally had more clout than the rest of us, was asked to step forward to receive a gift. The buzz in the crowd of some seventy or eighty Basuto indicated that to receive such a gift was a great honour, especially on Christmas Day. It dawned on us that the heavily uniformed presenter was their leader – he had to be the leader, as he was wearing more lavatory chains with handles than anyone else. He also pointed at the skyline with authority and made leader like noises. Someone had given him a chain to hold which had a sheep attached to the end. He beckoned towards Tim, obviously recognising a fellow leader, and then towards us. His speech was a little lengthy, but he did finish before the afternoon downpour. The essence of what he said was by now familiar to us, referring to our visit as a great tribute to someone, but never mentioned to whom it was. Queen Victoria was mentioned yet again, but the punchline was unusual and certainly unexpected. We were presented with the sheep as a Christmas present and expected to kill it, cook it, and eat it. Tim made a brief, but polite acceptance speech and led the sheep away to the slaughter. Tim's decorum, manners and 'clout' had got us through the day, and we handed the sheep to a local South African farmer who said he would look after it for us.

We did have a few meals with the farmer and his wife in the New Year, and I sometimes wondered if we had eaten our four-legged woolly Christmas present.

By mid-January we had completed the film, and apart from David upsetting some nuns by taking a bath halfway up a hillside, which overlooked the convent girls' school, and myself pulling a lavatory chain on the uniform of a visiting chief, who could have passed for an Air Vice-Marshal (circa 1930), I think we got under the wire with a reasonably clean sheet.

We discovered that a lasting impression had been made when, as we drove away from Mantsonyane, two Basuto children and the teacher shouted to us, 'Keep on diddlin'!'

Roots of Africa

One afternoon, while filming at Lake Rudolf with Richard Leakey, we noticed a light aircraft flying low over the lake. It flew past the camp heading north.

'That could be Root,' said someone.

When the plane was some distance from us it banked quite sharply, and lost altitude. After almost making a full turn it headed straight towards us, about six feet above the water.

'That is definitely Root,' said the same voice.

The Cessna landed on the dirt airstrip, and a man and woman climbed out. Both of them were extremely suntanned, lightly weathered, and looked remarkably athletic.

Alan Root and his wife Joan were introduced to us, and by the time we had settled ourselves in the mess tent, Benson had arrived with some tea.

On introduction to Alan one couldn't help but notice that bits of him were missing. When I say missing, I don't mean they were lost or had being misplaced. The index finger of his right hand was absent. Where most of us have a pointing bit, he had fresh air; I thought, Best say nothing.

Alan and I are about the same age, but apart from a shared sense of humour, that is where the similarity ended. Alan has a good head of hair. I do not. He is constructed of muscle and sinew (bar one finger). I tend to veer more towards soft white flab. Alan, we were told, had looked into the jaws of death on many occasions and shown no fear. I am the last in a long line of devout cowards, but forever grateful that my anatomy contains a full complement of index fingers.

The purpose of Alan's visit was to examine the possibility of Martin, David and myself helping him with a film he was making for Survival TV. He was filming wildlife from a hot air balloon and wanted to get some footage of him learning to fly the balloon, accompanied by a trained pilot. The three of us thought this sounded like a cracking good idea, and arrangements would be made for us to join Alan and Joan at their home by Lake Naivasha when we had completed the Leakey film.

Who knows, I thought, maybe some of Alan's derring-do could rub off on me?

Lake Naivasha

Naivasha is a small town 50 miles north-west of Nairobi, and a mile or so south-west of the town is Lake Naivasha. Alan and Joan had a wonderful home 70 yards from the lake shore with lawns and garden going right down to the water's edge. Around the back of the house were many outbuildings where vehicles, film equipment and the balloon were stored. In the grounds there was a spacious aviary and a fenced area where various injured or orphaned animals were kept.

A striped hyena with razor sharp teeth loped around behind the fence, but the stars of the show were a very young hippo called 'Sally' and an aardvark called 'Million'. Alan insisted the anteater was called Million after the song 'Aardvark a million miles for one of your smiles' – we weren't convinced.

Sally had the run of the house, moving fully loaded furniture containing humans, with effortless ease. If you weigh half a ton, leaning on an armchair housing a muscular David, moves the obstacle without effort and clears the route for a young hippo.

Hot air balloon trips in Africa usually happen at dawn when the air is cooler. At 5:30 a.m. we filmed the balloon being inflated, gas cylinders fitted, and all the usual checks that have to be made. Phil Donnington an instructor had flown in from the UK to teach Alan the basics of balloon flight.

It was decided that Alan and Phil would be fitted with radio microphones so I could sit at the bottom of the basket, and that would give Martin more freedom to film them during the flight. David was left with the recovery team, as there was no room for him in the basket.

The balloon ascended and Martin and I recorded Alan and Phil going through their routine. The odd thing about being at the bottom of the basket is there is nothing to indicate any kind of movement. All you can see is the burner, steel cables holding the basket to the balloon and the inside of the balloon itself.

Martin felt that what we had shot was okay and we would do some more filming of Alan attempting level flight. So when I stood up I had no idea how high we were or where. Phil thought we were at about 700 feet high and half a mile out over the lake. My intake of breath, stomach and wobbly legs agreed with him.

It was then that the burner went out.

'Do you have the matches?' asked Alan.

'No, I had a few when we lit the burner,' replied Phil.

We slowly started to descend.

'Have either of you two got any matches?' asked Alan.

We shook our heads.

'Where are the ones you had?' asked Phil.

'I've got those,' replied Alan, 'but they're damp.'

Our rate of descent had increased, and Phil reckoned we were at about 500 feet.

Alan connected a new gas cylinder to the burner and attempted to strike the damp matches.

By now the water appeared to be travelling towards us quite rapidly.

At about 250 feet Alan produced a spark sufficient for the burner to roar into life.

The continuous thunder of the burner was impressive, but not enough to slow us down.

We were now less than 100 feet from the water, and Martin was holding the camera at arm's length above his head. I managed to lift the recorder and radio receivers about chest high.

When we hit the water there was an impressive splash and the steel cables snapped tight as the weight of the basket, the cylinders and occupants was now shared with the water. The hot air was fortunately beginning to lift the balloon slightly and it stabilised with us waist deep in water, but sort of afloat.

The recovery team plus David had seen this action going on and had been following our route in two powerboats. Within a minute they were alongside to collect the crew and our equipment. As soon as Martin and I climbed into the rescue boats the balloon now had less to lift and slowly took to the air again with Phil and Alan wet but smiling.

The powerboat took us back across the lake to the house. David dried off the camera, which hadn't got very wet, and the film in the magazine was dry. Unfortunately, one could not say the same for the recorder, which had been totally dunked. It was the last job that machine would be doing for a couple of days.

I looked at the balloon in the distance, as it drifted towards Naivasha, and thought, Perhaps that's my introduction to derring-do, and it's only day one…

The Shadow of Kilimanjaro

After completing the filming in Lesotho, we flew to Kenya to work with Alan once again. The plan was to film some Masai warriors having a ride in Alan's hot air balloon at the Amboseli Game Reserve, and then move on to Mzima Springs in Tsavo National Park to film Alan and Joan swimming with hippos, and the occasional crocodile.

This kind of activity was all par for the course where Alan was concerned, but a trifle extreme, in my view.

The location at Amboseli had the appearance and feeling of a feature film. A dozen tents had been set up, under a cluster of acacia trees, facing the northern slopes of Mount Kilimanjaro. It was the sort of scene one fully expected Clark Gable or John Wayne to stride about proclaiming, 'There's gorillas in them thar hills.'

The first morning I woke about 5 a.m. to the sounds of men making the usual early morning noises men make early in the morning. Nothing strange about that – except there was. As well as the usual manly sounds there was also the sounds of tearing timber and rending foliage. Now Martin, David and I have been known to be acoustically excessive in the mornings, but never to this extent.

Somebody said in semi-hushed tones, 'Stay in your tents and be quiet.'

I looked through the mesh window of my tent and could just make out seven or eight elephants tearing long strips of bark from the trees of our camp. In the distance beyond the elephants, the first shaft of sunlight was turning the snow on the crater of

Kilimanjaro a deep pink. Clark Gable had to turn up soon.

Martin and Alan thought it best to shoot the action with the balloon and the Masai on as many cameras as was possible to cover whatever the unknown might offer. I was given a 16 mm clockwork Bolex camera and told I would be travelling with the Masai in a truck driven by Joan. Martin was to be in the balloon with Alan and as many Masai warriors as would fit in with them. David would operate another camera, from another vehicle.

Alan decided to wear a small microphone connected to a miniature recorder inside the basket, as the only sound he thought would be interesting was that from the Masai as they jumped from the moving truck driven by Joan into the balloon basket, which he would fly alongside the truck. Somebody asked if the Masai knew about this ruse, and the reply was that they didn't need to know as they were warriors and knew no fear.

We found a good stretch of reasonably flat ground in the Reserve, which covered a couple of miles. The weather was perfect with a light breeze to take the balloon along. A dozen warriors and I, plus Bolex, climbed into the truck driven by Joan. David was in the other vehicle about fifty yards away. The burner was roaring and the balloon gently lifted off.

The balloon was flying about twenty feet from the ground, Joan took our vehicle underneath the balloon and a Masai warrior prepared himself to jump. Alan brought the balloon down to the level of Joan who eased the vehicle about two feet away from the basket. I leant over the side of the truck and could see the warrior leaning out ready to jump. At a moment when the Masai knew it was now or never, he leapt from the truck and in seconds was inside the basket, smiling and laughing. Alan was burning the flame at full bore the moment the weight if the warrior was on the basket to avoid being pulled to the ground.

This had been a roaring success and the remaining Masai were anxious to join their warlike buddy.

We repeated this action until the basket contained nine laughing, excited Masai warriors, who looked from a distance like a silhouetted bunch of flowers. Alan was right about the sound, their shrieks and laughter was the only sound required.

The flight lasted another half-hour, and we followed the

balloon as the recovery team. Martin needed to get out of the basket so David could film Alan flying with the Masai without a 6'1" beefy Yorkshireman in the shot. Martin decided to do the reverse of what the Masai had done, so Alan brought the basket alongside our vehicle, Martin passed the camera to me, and then climbed onto the side of the truck. The problem was that Martin's muscular frame and bulk when not in the basket, caused the balloon to rise quickly away from the vehicle, and Martin took a bad fall. Fortunately, he landed a few feet away from the moving truck and not near the wheels.

Alan flew Martin to Nairobi Hospital, where he was checked over and found to be bruised, shaken, but declared indestructible.

Both returned the following day, and it was decided to shoot some 'gentle stuff' until Martin's aching limbs were behaving in a friendlier manner.

Mzima Spring

Those who have been attacked by a hippo are usually no longer with us to tell the tale. Alan is an exception.

Mzima Spring in Tsavo National Park is fed by rainwater being filtered through volcanic rock some forty miles away. This means the water is crystal clear and where it comes out of the rock is pure and wonderful to drink.

The spring, with its families of hippos, crocodiles, elephants and vervet monkeys, make it an ideal spot for safaris from nearby Kilaguni Lodge.

Our camp was set a short walk from the spring and hidden from the tourist trail.

Alan and Joan had filmed at the spring previously, and after various attempts to get good under-water footage of hippos and crocodile, discovered the only satisfactory method was to get into the water and swim alongside them with the camera. Alan assured us that they took no notice.

It was proposed that Alan and Joan would repeat this exercise and Martin would follow them, filming both them and the hippos. David and I would have a camera position overlooking the water and film any interesting action from there. Obviously as there was no sound to record I could take some stills, assist David and be a general gofer. This arrangement worked remarkably well and some great material was filmed in the first week.

Naturally, the obvious questions did go through our minds, What do we do if…?

Martin, always the positive one, remarked, 'Well, Keith has the medical kit, so we do have morphine, hypodermics, sutures, scalpels and bits.' This was said in a manner intended to fill all with confidence in my medical prowess. I could clean a cut and apply a bandage, but wasn't too sure of the procedure should Martin decide to annoy a crocodile having a 'bad hair' day.

A sequence Alan was keen to film was Joan scratching the buttocks of a hippo. We didn't say much but we did look at each other, and then at Joan, attempting to show her some concern, and our sincerest good wishes.

I was thinking, If you are really that bored with life, scratching the buttocks of a hippo weighing in at a couple of tons with jaws stronger than a JCB wouldn't be my first choice to relieve the tedium.

Alan did go on to explain that small fish come and eat the algae or bits that attach themselves to the hippo's buttocks, and Joan would simply be emulating the fish. The amazing thing was that Joan appeared happy to go along with this suggestion.

At first light the following morning we all mustered at the spring with cameras, tripods, underwater housings, breathing tanks and the medical kit.

Joan seemed quite at ease with what she was about to do, and was already swimming in the spring. David and I helped Martin into his wetsuit and strapped the air tanks to his back.

At least seven hippos were snorting and blowing in the middle of the spring, their large bodies clearly visible through the water. A few elephants were drinking at the far side, but we were unable to spot the two crocodiles, which I thought augured well.

By mid-morning, Martin had shot a couple of magazines and told us that Joan had performed her task perfectly, and they had another cracking sequence. He just needed to get two or three more close-ups of the hippos and that would do it. David fitted another magazine and Martin lowered himself under the water.

Alan and Joan were swimming in front of Martin in their usual formation, when David suddenly started throwing small stones into the water. I was some distance from David, but it looked to me as though he was attempting to hit Martin with the stones.

I called to him and asked him, 'What are you doing? You're going to hit him?'

'That's what I'm trying to do, the crocodile's in the water about ten feet behind him!'

We both picked up stones and threw them at Martin. Some of them landed in the water in front of the camera, and he told us later, he couldn't believe what the two lunatics on the bank were doing, they were ruining the shot.

We were now throwing small rocks, hoping to draw his attention to twenty feet of armoured terminator cruising behind him.

David and I were now desperate, then suddenly, what appeared to be an underwater eruption occurred right where they were filming a hippo. The water surged and the surge moved forward with a huge black grey back of a hippo breaking the surface, and then moving away. The crocodile turned away from the turmoil and disappeared.

Alan broke the surface, shouting, *'Joan – get out of the water – it's bitten me!'* Then he then disappeared under the water.

Martin dived down, grabbed Alan and swam with him, pulling him to the nearest bank.

David ran to Alan and Martin, and helped to lift Alan out of the water. He then grabbed the 6-foot 'bang stick' and offered one end to Joan to pull herself out of the spring, and away from the hippos. David then realised he had given Joan the explosive end to hold. It almost wasn't Joan's day either.

The 'bang stick' is a pole with a shotgun cartridge fitted to one end, together with a spring-loaded detonator. This can be rammed against the side of a croc or hippo and the explosion is supposed to deter them, not damage them.

I grabbed the much spoken-of medical kit, and hurried to the disaster area.

I got to them in less than a minute, only to find David had

torn a sleeve off his shirt and already had a tourniquet around Alan's thigh.

The hippo had bitten Alan through the calf muscle, and remarkably the bones had not been broken. It was a clean wound, as one could clearly see through the hole in his leg – about the size of a Coke bottle.

Every few minutes David was releasing the pressure on the thigh and allowing a flow of blood momentarily, then applying the tourniquet again.

I was fumbling in the medical kit looking for morphine capsules and a hypodermic needle. I must confess that up to this point I had never stuck a needle in anyone, I had only practised on a potato under the watchful eye of my father-in-law, who was a doctor. He had told me that in an emergency, just stick the needle into a thigh muscle or the buttocks whichever is available. The morphine is only to kill pain, as that is what puts people into a state of shock.

All this was rattling around in my head when a lady's voice said, 'I'm a nurse, and this man is a doctor.'

I thought, I'm hallucinating – or I'm in shock… It sounded like somebody just said there was a nurse and a doctor.

The lady repeated the information and I think I said something like, 'Good, you'll know what to do' – as if medical training always included treatment of the occasional hippo bite.

A safari coach had arrived, and as miracles go, just happened to have a doctor and a nurse on board. I passed an unopened hypodermic pack and a capsule of morphine to the 'doctor', stretching my belief to its limits that this total stranger really was a doctor, and watched as he injected the solution into Alan's thigh. So that's how it's done, I thought, it's nothing like the potato!

The safari guide told us there were two planes at the Kilaguni airstrip eight miles away, and one was due to leave for Nairobi at one o'clock.

We lifted Alan into the back of a truck and David handed him a full bottle of Glenfiddich whisky. I still don't know where he got it from, and I have learned never to ask. David and Martin climbed into the truck with him, David still releasing the tourniquet every so often. As they slowly drove away I was surprised Alan was so calm for someone who had just lost another part of his body. Maybe the morphine was working, or the whisky, or both?

I thanked the 'doctor' and the helpful lady, who were still amused and a little puzzled to find a film crew in the middle of Kenya with a medical kit containing morphine, sterilised hypodermics, sutures and the like – and not a medic among them.

I smiled, 'Well – these things do happen!'

They got on the coach and continued with their safari.

I sat on a rock and packed the medical kit away. A few of Alan's men were there clearing up various items, and loading the air tanks, flippers, and David's camera and tripod into a Range Rover. The reality of what had happened was slowly dawning on me, plus the miracle of Alan being alive. Martin told us later that the hippo had Alan in its jaws but the weight of the air tanks caused Alan to slide from the mouth, so when the jaws closed it was on his legs and not his body.

Looking at the hippos in the centre of the spring, all appeared calm, although they were grouped together as if ready to 'rumble'. As I stared across the clear water I noticed a white shape and a black shape with silver bits moving gently under the water. The shapes were some twelve to fifteen feet from the hippos.

Both underwater cameras were still in the spring, and I knew one of the housings had a slow leak.

I'd had enough derring-do for one day, so I looked around for a willing volunteer to go into the water and get them.

It's always amazing how people of any race or creed worldwide recognise the 'searching for a volunteer look' – and disappear!

There was a Park Ranger, but he wasn't going to get his uniform wet. After all, he had just seen what one of the hippos had done to Alan, and now there was a whole gang of them.

Nguri, one of Alan's right-hand men turned up and I approached him, expecting him to do a runner when he heard the words 'Do you think you could…?' – But he didn't. Perhaps that was why Alan had selected him to be his adjutant.

I suggested we should take the steel boat that Alan had used for underwater filming. It was like a 7-foot rectangular coffin with glass panels at one end. We would take the 'bang stick' with us to ward off any crocodiles or hippo that might be inquisitive. I would kneel in the front to reach the submerged cameras, and he could pole us out to them. He wasn't all that pleased with my idea but didn't say no.

The 'bang stick' was at the bottom of the boat with the cartridge by my knees, which was the most stupid place to stow it, as Nguri could have kicked it accidentally, triggered the detonator, and I would have lost both kneecaps.

I moved the explosive end of the bang stick away from my legs.

Nguri poled the steel 'coffin' very slowly towards the hippos. They grunted and blew water into a spray. I felt a bit nauseous, and Nguri said, 'We are going to die... both of us are going to die.'

This was something I didn't particularly want to hear right then. I reasoned that the hippos would have seen Alan filming from this metal coffin on quite a few occasions, so they probably knew it was friendly, providing he hadn't used the bang stick on one of their colleagues.

I quickly checked the bodies of the hippos for any bang stick damage. As I did this, two of them turned to look at me. Now I was trembling and feeling considerably nauseous.

I didn't know whether it was a good move or not, there are no rules written for what we were doing, but Nguri managed to get the vessel in between the hippos and the cameras, so when we leant over to pull them from the water we were not leaning towards the leviathans.

We got back to the bank with the cameras and Nguri now told me, 'I knew we would be alright, my grandfather was very friendly with hippos.'

I said nothing; I was still trembling.

Alan was in hospital for over a month, and recovering for the next six.

We returned to London and dined out on stories of man-eating hippos and feats of great daring. I didn't mention the nauseous and trembling bit.

Two in the Bush

The autobiographical film of the work in which Alan and Joan were involved, had taken much longer than either of them or Survival TV had intended. This was mainly due to the seasons and Alan recovering from the hippo attack.

Come autumn 1979, the weather and the seasons were right, and Alan was ready to complete the film. Martin and I left for Kenya; I think David was working on another job somewhere.

The first week we filmed close-ups of Alan's scarred leg, and an assortment of hippo teeth, plus various animal sequences in the garden at Naivasha. The second week was planned for travelling to some of the key locations needed to finish sequences, which would involve a considerable amount of driving.

Alan had two Range Rovers, a small truck and some smaller vehicles. It was decided that Martin would drive one of the Range Rovers and I would drive the other. Both were loaded to the gunnels and fitted with substantial trailers. A heavy generator had been fitted into my trailer and camping equipment into the other one.

Alan was to fly ahead and sort out the arrangements at the campsites and also to negotiate with some of the Game Wardens.

On route when Martin and I stopped for petrol he said that his steering seemed a bit sloppy, and asked what mine was like.

I told him, 'It seems a bit slow to respond, but we're towing quite a load and won't be going fast.'

We were heading for Narok on a typical African tarmac road. It was the end of the rains, and the soft dirt shoulder at the side of the road had been partly washed away, leaving a step down from the tarmac of nearly a foot. I was driving in front of Martin going down a moderate incline, and a lorry was coming up the gradient. I slowed down and pulled over to give the lorry plenty of clearance and the inside wheels of the Range Rover went down the step on to the soft shoulder.

After the lorry had passed I tried to bring the vehicle back on to the tarmac. The trailer began to weave in a sort of snake action as I tried again to get the Range Rover on to the road.

Fourteen days later I remember Martin and a nurse standing over my bed in Nairobi Hospital. Martin was talking to me but I can't remember what he was saying.

Martin told me much later that the Range Rover had rolled over four times and I had been thrown through the rear window. Quite a lot of me was damaged, and I spent the next two and half months under traction in the hospital. I was confused by not knowing whether I was in London or Nairobi, as most of the nurses were African or Asian and all spoke to me in English. I then confounded them by insisting I could prove I was in London by taking them in a taxi to see Nelson's Column in Trafalgar Square as soon as I was up and about. This seemed to amuse them, but it was another month before it dawned on me why they were amused.

I was now the third person to have worked on *Two in the Bush* and ended up in Nairobi Hospital!

The film was finally finished, and almost a year later transmitted by Survival TV. On the day of transmission, David and his wife decided to spend the entire day in bed and watch the programme from the safety of their duvet. David was the only crew member who hadn't been admitted to hospital during the making of the film, and he was taking no chances.

Gorillas in the Mist

In the late Eighties Alan was back in Nairobi Hospital yet again.

David and I received the news while waiting for 'the call of the wild' to take us into Tanzania with him.

We knew he was filming wild gorillas in Rwanda for Warner Brothers' *Gorillas in the Mist* and had almost completed what was required by Hollywood, when he came across a very young gorilla that let him get quite close. In typical Alan style, he got closer and closer until the father of junior gorilla thought enough is enough. Father gorilla was a 25-stone silverback in peak condition, and came at Alan sideways on all fours. When a silverback approaches you in this manner he is no longer being polite.

Father gorilla picked Alan up, bit him in the thigh, and threw him some fifteen feet into the forest. The silverback then went to check on junior just in case he needed to come and slap Alan around a bit more.

Alan was working with his assistant Bruce Davidson, and somehow the two managed to get down the mountain to their transport, and to a hospital.

After skin grafts and more convalescence, Alan flew David and myself to the Serengeti where we helped him to complete his current wildlife film and geographical study.

The memories I share with Alan Root are simply remarkable. Working alongside him in the dense rainforest of Zaire on the Epulu River with some local tribes, or living up a tree with him for ten days in the Central African Republic, are events that have shaped and influenced my life.

It's hard to close a chapter on Alan, but I believe what was once said of him is true:

> *'Alan is probably among the last of those people who perceive the total vastness of Africa and see it as a metaphor for freedom.'*

NB   Alan Root's index finger was amputated in the late Sixties after he was bitten by a deadly snake.

Blatant Name-dropping

Elizabeth Taylor

By July of 1980 I had been in love with Elizabeth Taylor for twenty-four years. There was no doubt in my mind that should we ever meet she would be aware of the intense passion I felt for her. Now I did realise at the time there was a slight inconvenience in the shape of R Burton, this did not, however, quell my feelings for the lady. Her performance in *The Taming of the Shrew* in glorious colour to the stark black and white of *Suddenly Last Summer* only served to cement my passion more permanently.

The intensity of my joy was impossible to measure when I received a phone call from Martin to ask if I was free to work on a documentary film on the making of the feature film *The Mirror Cracked*. The stars of the film were Tony Curtis, Rock Hudson, Kim Novak, and – joy upon ecstasy – Elizabeth Taylor (without R Burton). I believe Angela Lansbury had a part in the film but it was of no matter.

Come day one of the shoot and Martin, David and I arrived on set in plenty of time to set up and look around. Our director told us that as the shot the studio were setting up was a little involved, we would not be doing any interviews until the afternoon, so we should stay out of the way and pick up some studio atmosphere during the takes by the main unit.

Tony Curtis, in the meantime, had made himself known, as he was aware we would be interviewing him the following day. He is friendly, charming and incredibly funny, and he does the most wonderful impression of Cary Grant.

With the general melee on the main set, and dozens of technicians attending to the finest detail it is often difficult to notice the arrival of some major stars. So it was this morning. Elizabeth Taylor was already sitting on the edge of the bed on the set and chatting to the director. I knew that even at a distance of some 60 to 70 feet she must have been feeling the intensity of passion travelling towards her from the documentary sound recordist. I felt sure the deep warmth that was passing through her must have been giving her immense, yet uncertain pleasure. She, of course, being a true professional of some years, was able to disguise the emotional turmoil that was vibrating through her, and carry on with her acting career.

The scene that was about to be shot by the main unit was a tricky one regarding the timing, which I will attempt to explain. Elizabeth Taylor and her male lead actor were to be kneeling on the bed facing each other. The action in the story took place in a 1940s film studio, so a dummy 35 mm film camera on a 1940s tracking dolly would be moving around the end of the bed from right to left, with actors playing the crew and the director. The real 35 mm film camera shooting the feature film would be on separate tracks behind the dummy camera, and would track round with it, keeping Elizabeth Taylor and co-star plus the dummy camera and acting crew in their shot. Our director, Iain, thought it would make a jolly good shot for our 16 mm documentary camera to track round behind the other two cameras and therefore show Elizabeth Taylor, co-star, dummy camera plus crew, and real 35 mm camera plus real crew. We had no tracks; this meant Martin walking round behind the main unit and handholding the camera, with me slightly behind him and to his right side. I had no problem with this arrangement, as it took me at least twenty feet closer to Elizabeth Taylor, and I felt sure she would feel the intensity of my presence.

The first assistant director called for 'red light and bell', which means the main action is about to be filmed, and when anyone hears that bell and observes the red light, they know that if they fancy keeping their job they will stay quiet. The first assistant called for sound to turnover and for the main 35 mm camera to run, the clapper loader marked the shot with the clapperboard and the first assistant handed over to the director, who said quietly to Elizabeth Taylor, 'In your own time, Elizabeth.'

As she started her lines, the cameras slowly tracked from right to left, and Martin and I walked silently around behind them, my heart was pounding; *she* was speaking. As we tracked round we had just passed what must have been the halfway mark when *she* turned her head to the left and looked past the dummy camera, past the main 35 mm camera and, with those penetrating lilac blue eyes, locked her gaze on to mine and in a harsh American accent shouted, '*Get that creep out of my eye line!*'

I was devastated. The main unit director called, 'Cut' and the shot was reset. Meanwhile I had disappeared behind some scenery. Our director came to find me and said, 'That was terrific, they are going again. Go and get the next one.' I told him I was not going anywhere near the set and I would cover it from the side. They were still resetting, and my shattered feelings and thoughts were busy attempting to construct a rescue package. How could I possibly approach her now?

The call for 'red light and bell' brought everyone into gear and we were off again. All was going well until about the halfway mark when Liz Taylor looked past the dummy camera, past the 35 mm camera, past Martin and shouted, 'Get that creep out of my eye line!'

I looked out from behind the safety of the scenery flat and thought, Oh joy, oh wonder, such relief – it's all part of the script! In the shadows behind Martin stood Kim Novak, the true recipient of the line. My breathing became easier but my feelings were shattered. Perhaps R Burton could handle that firepower. I decided it was best left to him.

HRH Princess Margaret

In the late Sixties Lord Snowdon had been making a documentary programme with the BBC, and he happened to mention to the sound recordist that he would like some information on sub-miniature microphones. The recordist mentioned my name, as he knew I had a few sub-miniature microphones, and he gave Lord Snowdon my number.

I was taken aback to receive a phone call from a lady in Kensington Palace who just happened to be Lord Snowdon's secretary.

She explained the situation, and asked that if I had the time, could I pop in to Kensington Palace with a few samples of the 'said items' and show them to her boss.

Now, a lad from the north doesn't get too many offers like

Blatant Name-dropping

this, and so with a few of the 'said items' I arranged to pop by and drop them in. The curiosity in me wanted to have a look inside the premises occupied by Lord Snowdon and his gorgeous wife, known to all as HRH Princess Margaret.

In my total naivety, and gullible imaginings, I believed this could be just around the corner from a knighthood, if all went well.

I got there, popped in, saw Snowdon, gave him 'said items', and left.

The very next day, I got a second phone call from Lord Snowdon's secretary, who thanked me for popping in, as I was passing, but if I just happened to be passing again, could I do likewise. With the knighthood now looming larger, I told her I could.

The second visit to Kensington Palace revealed a different situation. Lord Snowdon had in his study a stunning set of shelves. These, as you can imagine, were no ordinary shelves. Lord Snowdon at that time worked for the British Design Council, and naturally he had designer shelves as befitting. These shelves were something Laurence Llewellyn-Bowen would never have come across or even imagined, and they most certainly were not made from MDF. The shelves contained a battery of hi-fi equipment, a 16 mm projector, a tape recorder, and a gamut of sound equipment any audio enthusiast would love to own. The only problem with it was, that whilst each individual item worked perfectly, when each item was required to work together, it was found to be difficult. When I say difficult, perhaps one should say – silent!

Lord Snowdon asked me, very politely, if I knew of anyone who could fix the silent system, and whilst they were at it, could they install a tasteful unit, which would automatically switch all systems on at the correct time, and in the correct order.

With the knighthood now firmly fixed on the horizon, I said, 'Of course.' Knowing full well I wasn't going to let anyone else get their hands on this one – it was mine, all mine!

One afternoon the following week I was attempting to sort out the spaghetti configuration of wiring coming through the skirting board into Snowdon's study. The secretary had told me that there

Blatant Name-dropping

was only the staff in the palace, as the family was all away, so I had the place to myself. Most of the wires coming through the skirting board were from the huge sitting room, which was adjacent to the study.

I was lying flat on my stomach, with my head under the bottom designer shelf surrounded by a mess of cables, when the study door opened. From carpet level I could only make out a pair of lovely suntanned legs covered from the knee up by a smart turquoise dress. My first thought was she must be one of the house staff; I then managed to turn my head through the wires, and to my surprise recognised the face of Princess Margaret. I had been told Princess Margaret was on holiday in the Caribbean, but that information I rapidly began to doubt.

I wasn't sure what the correct procedure was, after all I had never been in the presence of a princess before, with my head covered in her husbands cables, and half of me under his bottom shelf.

I decided I'd best bow, and say something akin to 'Hello, m'aam, I'm just fixing your husband's wires'.

As I thought this, I realised that bowing from a lying position could become ungainly, but time was passing, and no gesture of humble respect had been made.

I thought go for it, and as my bottom rose into the air, I head-butted the floor. Realising how ridiculous this must look as an act of homage and royal respect, I went into press-up mode to recover the situation, and brought the back of my head into contact with the bottom designer shelf. I was now in modest pain and attempted to withdraw from the unfortunate position, only to find some of the wires wrapped round my neck.

'Are we in some difficulty?' asked the princess, who had come into the study.

'No m'aam, we'll be fine,' I replied.

Somehow I managed to reverse and escape the wires, find my feet, and perform an adequate impression of a genuflect, which probably looked more like a curtsey.

We both stood and looked at the mess of cables, when Princess Margaret pointed out to me that since the wires had been 'rearranged', the gramophone in the sitting room had ceased to

Blatant Name-dropping

work, and did I think it possible to fix that problem before tackling Lord Snowden's more extensive electronic investigation?

The sister of the Queen was standing next to me – I couldn't believe it. If my mother, who is an ardent royalist, could have seen what her lad was up to, she too would not have believed it.

The knighthood was now getting closer.

'Of course, m'aam, it shall be attended to,' and I went through the gesture of searching for a missing forelock.

After two more visits armed with a soldering iron I had sorted out the cables, and was on the final straight with the gramophone. That particular day was a Saturday, and Viscount Linley told me that they had been to see the film *Chitty Chitty Bang Bang* the previous afternoon. He also told me that one of the staff had gone to buy a record of the soundtrack, so they could play it later on for some friends who were coming for tea.

I explained to him that the gramophone wasn't quite ready for music, but I would try my best to fix it in time for his friends.

He assured me that he understood my situation, and alternative arrangements could be made to entertain his friends. I was taken aback.

I thought, Now there's breeding, a six-year-old putting a twenty-nine year old at his ease...

Just before lunch, the record arrived, and the soldering iron had performed it's magic. In a few moments the sitting room was filled with the music of *Chitty Chitty Bang Bang*. Lady Sarah and Viscount Linley ran into the room with their mother close behind. They held hands, forming a small circle and danced around singing to the music.

I watched, and smiled with relief, when once again I was taken aback. The children each held out a hand, and pulled me into the circle. We danced around and around, singing and laughing, well, the children were singing, Princess Margaret was singing, and I was looking polite, but dancing nevertheless.

Mother dear, if you could see me now. Holding hands with royalty and dancing... well – dancing of sorts.

It took four more visits to complete the 'electronic investigation', but on the way, I had the pleasure of rigging a couple of microphones to help Princess Margaret accompany herself at the grand piano in the sitting room, with a belting rendition of 'My Father was the Keeper of the Eddystone Light'.

The 'tasteful' switching unit for Lord Snowdon's sound system was fitted into the study. Princess Margaret sent me a beautiful photo of herself, taken by her husband, with a thank-you note for fixing the gramophone. But I guess the memory that stays with me, is the wonderful expression on the faces of her children as they danced to the sounds of *Chitty Chitty Bang Bang*.

Carroll Baker

London, 1964: *The Carpetbaggers*, a feature film starring Carroll Baker was to be premiered in Leicester Square, and the star of the film was expected to attend.

RAI, Italian Television, had asked Michael Colomb and myself to turn up at the hotel where Miss Baker was staying, and record a couple of minutes with her for their *Film Night* programme the following day.

This was the first premiere I had been to, and although it wasn't E Taylor or S Loren, I could make do with Carroll Baker.

Michael and I got to the hotel and met the Italian cameraman, who told us we were only doing the interview and not going to Leicester Square, as we wouldn't get near. The theatre was apparently already heaving with press.

We were told by the 'heavies' looking after Miss Baker that she would be down in five minutes, and she could only give us a couple of minutes for the interview as she was running a bit late. Our Italian director knew better than to enter into conversation with the American 'muscle', and smiled a diplomatic smile.

Michael told me that on these occasions he usually fitted a personal microphone on the star and the cameraman framed the shot with only the head and shoulders; this way the microphone wasn't in shot. Being an eager young assistant and ready to learn, I got the microphone from its box, and prepared myself for a close encounter with Miss Baker.

Voices were heard in the corridor and a lady entered the room accompanied by more American heavies.

'I don't want anyone getting near Miss Baker's dress – it's fragile,' was the first thing I heard her say.

Blatant Name-dropping

I looked at Michael, and he looked at me and smiled. He is a nice man.

The next moment Carroll Baker arrived, wearing what looked to me like – very little; but what she was wearing shone and glittered from top to bottom. No Italian cameraman worth his lens cap was going to frame that image simply head and shoulders – he'd be going for the full 'gazonka' as it was then known.

I looked at Michael again. He said, 'Get the "stick" microphone and a long cable, I'll find a chair.'

I wasn't sure what the chair was for, but I got the microphone and cable. I turned to find Michael, but he had gone. It's surprising how quickly panic comes upon one in those situations.

Michael returned to the room with a chair and walked towards Miss Baker. Nobody was surprised when two extra large 'heavies' moved in and took the chair from him.

He explained to the American gentlemen that the chair was for me to stand on next to Miss Baker.

That was the first I had heard of this arrangement, 'I can't do that,' I said. 'She's virtually naked!'

For some reason we had no microphone boom with us, so I was to be the human boom.

I climbed on to the chair by the side of Miss Baker and noticed for the first time she was actually fully clothed except for her bare arms.

A full-length skin-coloured fine mesh covered her body, and onto the mesh had been fastened clusters of diamonds and pearls. The gems had been most strategically placed, to gain clearance from the Lord Chamberlain's office, and were now only a couple of feet from my knees.

I stretched out my arm holding the 'stick' microphone as steadily as I was able, with one of the world's most beautiful women at my feet, and seven of the world's supreme heavies waiting to rearrange my anatomy at any given opportunity.

Miss Baker smiled at me and said, 'Hello big boy, you okay up there?' I nodded and blushed. The director asked her about the movie.

Fortunately, it was all over in two minutes, as my arm was beginning to tremble. Everyone said 'Thank you' and all left the room.

'Well, that wasn't too bad, was it?' said Michael with a smile. He is a nice man.

I always made sure we had a boom with us in future; a chap can only take so much pulchritude.

Ursula Andress

Our paths finally crossed on the set of *Clash of the Titans*. We were again making a documentary covering the production of the film, laced with the regular interviews.

Ursula Andress was playing the part of Aphrodite (who else!) and the costume designer had thought it best to fit her in a diaphanous dress with all the necessary plunges back and front. Martin quite naturally wanted to film Miss Andress full length, and again I was in the situation of not having anywhere to hide a microphone.

Martin and Iain Johnstone our director were chatting about framing and questions, I supposed, so I took the opportunity of approaching Aphrodite.

I gestured to Miss Andress with the miniature microphone, which was about the size of a baked bean, and said, 'Do you think I could possib… Er, I was hoping to attach… If I could slip this down… Would you be happy if…?'

I realised I was gibbering, and any semblance of cohesion had long since left the stage.

Miss Andress was remarkably patient and said quietly, 'You wish to place the microphone on my body?'

'I would like to, please – if you don't – mind I could – possibly if you were to – but then – I'll just get some…'

'The microphone will show through the dress,' she said.

'Yes, it most certainly will.' I smiled hesitantly, made a half-bow, and backed away.

I approached Martin and said, 'The microphone will show through the dress.'

'Yes, I know, I thought you were using the gun mic,' he said.

'Oh, I will, I will!' I replied, feeling relieved.

As we left Shepperton Studios in Martin's Volvo, I justified my mental quagmire with a consoling thought. It's not every day a chap gets to be within touching distance of Aphrodite – and fell asleep on the back seat.

Others Best Not Mentioned

A Bridge Too Far directed by Richard Attenborough and produced by Joseph E Levine was made in Holland in the mid-Seventies. The film contained more major world stars than you could shake a stick at.

Sean Connery, Dirk Bogarde, Michael Caine, Anthony Hopkins, Liv Ullmann, Gene Hackman, Robert Redford, Laurence Olivier, Ryan O'Neal, Elliott Gould, James Caan, Edward Fox, and a whole gamut of other famous faces. The intrepid trio were with them on and off for over three months.

Now that's 'unashamed name dropping – not to mention blatant.'

Sophia Loren

By the autumn of 2002, the springtime of my senility had passed unnoticed, except by close members of the family, and still there had been no sight of Sophia Loren. Oh hum!

Billy Joel

The world tour Billy Joel and his band had undertaken in 1987 was planned to finish in Russia. It was a time when Gorbachev and his government were offering access to Russia and a freedom not previously known. The birth of glasnost was under way.

Billy Joel and his team decided it would be the right time for them to make a documentary of the visit to Moscow and Leningrad.

In 1983 Martin and I had shot a film on street kids in Seattle, and on its release the following year it received massive press coverage both in the States and the UK. Billy Joel remembered having seen *Streetwise* and asked his people to find out who had made the film.

Martin got the phone call while we were shooting a film in LA

Blatant Name-dropping

in the spring of '87, and we both felt this could only be a good one to do.

Billy Joel's people met Martin in New York, and later we all met up in London. The plan was, that a commercial video would be made of the actual concerts, by a separate crew shooting on six 35 mm cameras. We would concentrate purely on covering Billy, his wife Christie Brinkley and their little daughter, Alexa Ray.

It became apparent, almost immediately; that the usual three-person crew was not going to be sufficient; extra muscle was required.

David was working in Australia with his wife Gill, so Martin took Jo Hidderley with him as assistant and second cameraman. Jo is an unusual film technician. Firstly, and probably the most important, you can work with him day in and day out in strange locations for a month and a half, and not want to kill him at any time. Secondly, he is one of these people with a permanent sense of good humour, but never tedious. On top of this he is a good cameraman, a terrific stills photographer, and apparently grows terrific 'wacky baccy' in his loft.

My choice was Graham Paddon, a soundman I had known for over twenty years, and as far as I know, we have never wanted to kill each other, or maybe Graham is just very polite.

The Hotel National in Moscow was the largest in Europe with 6,000 rooms. This may be small change to regular world travellers, but I got lost twice trying to find a room where one could get some breakfast.

Tiblisi in Georgia was one of our first locations, where it had been arranged to film a local singing group in a thirteenth-century monastery, and also to travel into the mountains an hour away to meet a centenarian choir.

For some unknown reason the people who live at altitude in these mountains often live to be over a hundred-years-old. Doctors are divided on their reasons for this longevity. Some think it's the air quality, combined with diet; others think exercise and taking the waters. Whatever the reason, the twelve men who turned up in uniform to sing and to dance for us were one-hundred-years-old plus some.

Custom in these mountains is to provide some form of meal

for visitors from abroad, and this was to be no exception for the centenarians and their wives. After the filming we were taken to a small village high in the mountains where a most splendid banquet had been prepared.

A further custom is that the meal can only begin when the chief centenarian drinks some wine from a special horn and tells us to begin eating.

It was noticed that the numbers of uniformed centenarians had increased and joined their brothers on the main table.

The first ritual after the wine from the horn, is to propose a toast. An old man got to his feet, said something, which sounded happy, raised his goblet and drank the lot – we were told to do likewise. When someone asked if we had to drink the lot, our interpreter told us if we only drank half the wine only half of the toast would be fulfilled.

The wine was deep red and rough, but so very tasty. It was their local brew, which was left buried under the ground for two years.

Someone was explaining about the origins of the wine in the horn before the meal when another toast was proposed. We were on our feet, the goblet was emptied and everything seemed grand.

Jo Hidderley was saying he thought the wine was probably about 15% proof when the toast routine happened again.

I asked Jo, 'Who is filling the goblets?'

He said, 'I don't know, but they are always full.'

As the atmosphere became more jovial, not that it had been lacking on that front, the food arrived. It looked wonderful, tasted delicious, but nobody knew what it was. There was red meat, a lot of red meat. There was dark brown meat, and some more brown meat, but almost black. Some fish-looking things turned up with some kind of vegetable mash that had red things stuck in the top.

It was all completely unknown, but wonderful.

'That's boar,' said a man's voice with some certainty.

'I thought it more the colour of wolf,' said another man, with even more authority.

The man with the horn was on his feet again; he looked cheerful, said something loudly, and downed a hornfull. A pleasing sensation had us on our feet, sinking another goblet of red to who knows who.

Blatant Name-dropping

I am not quite sure what happened next, but someone told me later I was on my feet, having realised it was my brother Andrew's birthday, and my arm was outstretched holding a loaded goblet. The voices quietened, and I proclaimed loudly 'Happy Birthday – Brother Andy'. In a split second, a row of uniformed men, whose collective ages came to more than 2,000 years, were on their feet, goblets in the air, shouting what sounded like 'Brudder Andrich'. Everybody cheered and I sat down.

The next morning all seemed a lot clearer, and we flew back to Moscow.

The three concerts in Moscow were completely brilliant, with each a total sell-out, and Billy Joel lifting the roof at virtuoso level. When he hit them with the Beatles number 'Back in the USSR', as someone said, 'The audience went ballistic.'

On one of the days we were taken to see the memorial to Vladimir Visourski. Like you, I had never heard of him before, but our interpreter told us he was a forerunner of glasnost, and in some way paved the way for Gorbachev with the people.

As we drove to the memorial, a queue of people had formed along the side of a park. 'That's the queue for Visourski,' said our man. 'They wait like that every day.'

The people in the queue varied greatly. Old people, young families with children, teenagers, and quite bizarrely, four brides still in their wedding gowns with new husbands and some of their guests.

The queue was almost two miles long and it was anticipated that any bride joining the queue now would have to wait at least two hours before she got to her reception.

Billy Joel asked the interpreter to explain all this.

Vladimir Visourski was a poet who wrote about the people of Russia, their hope of freedom, and their longing to share the free spirit of the world. He thought the best method to contact the people was to do it in song. Unfortunately, he couldn't sing or play the guitar very well, but the words were so powerful the people loved him, and still do. His poems are sung all over Russia.

When we got to the memorial it was nothing spectacular, just a bust of his head and shoulders with the frets of a guitar. The bust simply rested on the ground, and came to about knee height. Many framed photos of him, some candles in glass jars, and hundreds of flowers surrounded this. It was a perfect shrine for the poet of the people.

We filmed a memorable sequence at the memorial, and I suspect most of us came away visibly moved.

A week later we flew to Leningrad, which was totally different. The number of palaces and regal buildings, plus magnificent churches, was almost overwhelming.

We arrived at our hotel in the evening. The hotel had been a palace occupied by the Tsar's family, but long since converted. Checking in was always a major feat for any production manager. Billy Joel's contingent of one hundred a forty took some housing, and our meagre fifteen didn't help any.

That particular evening took about two hours and by the time everyone was housed it must have been ten o'clock.

Everyone… except me! A room had not been booked in my name.

I thought, This is a big place, they must have somewhere, after all I'm not very large.

As our American production team were sorting out the problem, I was standing by my pile of metal boxes looking hopeful, when I noticed a blonde woman in a smart turquoise suit walking towards me.

She came up to me and said, 'Hello.'

I said, 'Hello,' which I thought was only polite.

'Can I help you with anything?' she said in good English.

'I'm with these men,' I replied, pointing towards the reception, 'They are helping me find a room.'

She smiled a most beautiful smile and said, 'But I have a room.'

She really was most attractive, one could almost say 'pleasing'.

'My room will be plenty for you and all your lovely boxes.'

Lovely boxes, I thought, *I've never seen them as lovely, heavy yes, but never lovely…*

'My name is Katrina,' she said with that lovely smile. 'What is yours?'

Blatant Name-dropping

I was just about to tell her, only to be polite of course, when the production manager came up and told me they had found me a room for me in the old wing, if I didn't mind.

I turned to let Katrina know that I now had a room, but she had vanished.

'Who was that?' asked the production manager.

'Her name is Katrina, she told me I could share with her if there wasn't any other room.'

'Sure she did,' he said in his strong Bronx accent. 'Broads like that don't come on strong with guys like you.'

I thought, Yank – just watch your lip, I could easily get my dander up.

Russian hotels in the Eighties usually had a manager on each floor. This was often a woman sitting at a modest table surrounded by paperwork. If you required anything or had any complaints, this was the person to whom you would mention your grievance.

The lady responsible for the calm on the floor my room was situated wouldn't have received too many complaints. She was built like a prop forward for Bradford Northern and could certainly have shot put for the USSR Olympic team – you could only wonder about her mother.

As the hotel porter led us towards the 'prop forward', I noticed the elegant shape of Katrina in her turquoise suit standing by her.

Stack me, I thought, this is all I need.

'Hello,' said Katrina.

I said, '*Spazeba*.' I don't know why I did, but somebody had said, 'Always thank the Russians for everything, after all they were our allies.'

Right at that moment, World War II wasn't foremost in my thoughts, but only to get to my room without suffering any physical contact with 'Olga the Mighty'.

We turned a corner and entered a far more elaborate corridor than the one we had just left. I should point out that we had now been walking for about ten minutes, and still no sign of a room for the night.

Two more turns and we came to some ornate double doors. The porter stopped and produced an equally ornate key, which fitted the lock and opened the door. He pushed the large door open and beckoned me to come in. He was smiling. He switched the light on, but I couldn't see anything to smile about.

The room was about twenty feet square, carpeted, but with no bed or furniture, only some coat hooks on one wall and two more large doors opposite.

The porter walked towards the doors and opened one. He entered the darkness and put on some lights in the next room. I followed him into the room, and stood with my mouth open. The production manager was right behind me and simply said, 'Heavens to Betsy!'

The room must have been fifty feet by forty feet, with three huge double windows on the far wall. It was heavily carpeted, and furnished with three large sofas', four or five armchairs and one beautiful dark wood table surrounded by eight matching chairs. Cabinets and small tables were placed around the room by the walls, magnificent oil paintings were hung in splendid gold frames, and the whole room was lit by two stunning crystal chandeliers, supplemented by a few correctly placed table lamps.

Impressive as this all is, there was still no sign of a bed or a bathroom, and all I wanted to do was get some sleep.

'This is alright?' asked the porter. I smiled and nodded.

'Follow, this way,' he said.

Yet another door was opened to reveal a room of almost similar size, but with two huge double windows. Against one wall was a colossal bed with a large painting over it, which could have been Katrina's mother. A couple of modest sofas plus two armchairs and some cabinets and a colossal dressing table completed the furnishings. This room was also lit with a breathtaking chandelier.

'This is okay?' asked the porter.

'This will be most satisfactory,' I think I said, now warming to the occasion.

You have probably guessed. The bathroom was vast with a solitary seven-foot bath set in the centre on black and white tiles. The ornate lavatory was so far away that it went into perspective, and in an emergency one would have to allow ample time to cover the distance.

Ten minutes later I had stripped off and was having a good wash, when there was a loud knocking from somewhere in the distance. I grabbed a towel and headed out of the bathroom towards the knocking, which was still coming for a considerable distance. Fortunately, I had left a couple of the table lamps on in the sitting room, but when hurrying towards distant knocking wrapped only in a towel, one could do with more than just a couple of lamps. Toe stubbing was inevitable. The knocking continued.

I banked over, negotiating a small table and an expensive cabinet, and coming out of the bend, hit the final straight past the coat hooks.

I unlocked the door and there stood Katrina, still looking elegant in her turquoise suit.

'Don't you ever go to bed?' I said, hanging on to my towel. 'It's midnight.'

'Yes, but you forgot your lovely boxes.' She was absolutely right, I had completely forgotten my 'lovely boxes'.

Behind her were two porters who had brought all the cases to my 'palace' and Katrina had offered to show them where I was.

They pushed their baggage trolley into the lobby area and unloaded the cases. I avoided helping them, due to slipping towel syndrome and bare toes. I gestured that I had no money to tip them, and apologised, but I did remember to say '*Spazeba*' and gave a half-bow. I don't know why.

They left – and to my relief, Katrina followed them. She said, 'Goodnight, Englishman,' and gave me a gentle smile.

The following day, my assistant, Graham, was taken ill with appendicitis and taken to Visitor Hospital No.2. That evening I spent over six hours trying to telephone Graham's wife in London to give her the news. It did seem totally incongruous to be sitting in more opulent surroundings than I could ever have envisaged, trying to use a phone that didn't work.

Billy Joel was taking Leningrad by storm and being recognised all over the city. I suppose having a film crew in tow did draw attention to whatever he did.

A group of teenagers who had been to one of the concerts saw him by a canal, and in their excitement could hardly speak.

'It's you, it really is you!'

'We were at your concert.'

'It was great.'

Billy shook hands with each of them and nodded his appreciation.

'It's really you – Billy Joel – here – by a canal in Leningrad!'

Billy smiled, and with his wry 'New York state of mind' said, 'Everybody has to be somewhere.'

For those kids on the edge of glasnost, that was about the most enlightening remark they had ever heard.

It was our last day in Leningrad. The crew and Billy felt that we couldn't leave the city without visiting the Hermitage Museum.

We only had a 'window' in the day of just over an hour (I'd never heard that expression before) but I got the feeling we had to be quick.

Someone said, probably Jo Hidderley, he had read in a guidebook on Leningrad, that if one spent thirty seconds looking at every item in the Hermitage it would take about ten weeks to see everything in the museum.

We didn't have that time, so we jogged the Hermitage in 45 minutes.

Visitor Hospital No.2 did a good job on Graham. Even if the stitches did look like steel hawsers, they were not going to come out in a hurry. And he did fly to London on Billy Joel's private flight.

I sent a postcard from Leningrad telling all – 'Billy Joel is a life-changing force.' You come away from him feeling better with life. I still believe that; I saw it happen to many people.

Madonna

Carrie Britton, an educated and intelligent lady, wanted Chris Morphet 'the cameraman' and Luther K Desmond to shoot a half-hour documentary with her. One could immediately say that doubt had to be cast on her 'education and intelligence' by the very choice of crew she had requested.

Blatant Name-dropping

The film she had in mind was to follow a couple of paparazzi around the West End trawling for work. This sounded like the kind of work Morphet and Desmond excelled in, and unanimously said, 'You bet, lead us to it.'

Hugh Thompson and Phil Loftus were not what we expected. For starters, they both had integrity and a moral base from which they worked. These guys were not your regular paparazzi. They were easy to be with, they were likeable people.

Hugh told us, 'I have no problems taking pictures of any famous person in the street, that's public property. They've made their names using the media, now it's time to give a little back. If a famous lady was sunbathing topless in her back garden, I wouldn't take the picture, that's private, that's not public property, but if she's in the street then that's fair game.'

We trawled the streets with them around Soho – theatre land – fancy restaurants – and the premiere of a feature film, *The Fugitive* at the Warner in Leicester Square.

Hugh was in a 'press pen' one side of the cinema entrance with Carrie, Morphet and Desmond, Phil was on the other side with Carlo.

It was a good evening for Hugh, as most of the *big* names came to his side. I shall only mention a few to highlight the passing of time.

Clint Eastwood, he looked great, he's ten years older than I am, but looks ten years younger.

Gary Glitter arrived with an unknown Amazonian young woman. His hair was black on black, attempting to look part of an earlier life. It was sad.

Bob Geldof turned up with wife Paula Yates. They both smiled politely, and Hugh's motor drive rattled off a few shots; he was sort of pleased.

A most determined yet striking woman with short dark hair walked positively into the theatre and shouted at someone in the press pen 'Don't bug me – I'm out of oestrogen and I have a gun!'

Jerry Hall was on her own when she arrived and looked stunning. She paused for the press and smiled – now she looked even more stunning.

A footballer with attitude arrived with his wife, and looked ordinary, nobody took his picture; it was of no matter.

A black Daimler pulled up and Princess Diana stepped out. The battery of flash bulbs must have resembled the Western Front. She looked breathtaking, beautiful and so very lovely. Everyone was shouting, people were screaming. The chap from the *Daily Express* shouted, 'It's me Di, one for me, Di, one for me, Di!' Someone else shouted, 'Di, Di, over here Di!' I thought, I'll join in, she knows me: 'Hello, Royal Highness, you made me tea at Highgrove – remember?' – I don't think she remembered. She must have made a lot of tea at Highgrove.

Hugh was pleased, he had some good shots of Princess Di, and enough of the others to have made it worthwhile. Phil came over looking happy; they had both got some good stuff.

A couple of nights later Madonna was due to attend a party at the ICA in the Mall. Hugh had decided to cover this while Phil lurked outside San Lorenzo's in Beauchamp Place hoping to get a few shots of the great and the good.

At midnight there was no sign of Madonna and the paparazzi who were there hadn't taken any shots of anyone arriving at the ICA. The general feeling was, Madonna probably wouldn't be turning up and everyone else was too boring.

We had been shooting film of almost anyone who had arrived – just in case.

A large limo headed slowly towards us and Carrie said, 'It must be her, turn over quickly!'

We turned over, and tried to see who was in the car. We also noticed that the paparazzi were quiet and the usual racket of motorised shutters was not apparent.

Three members of a 'seedy and inadequate pop group' climbed out of the limo, and hurried into the ICA.

Carrie told us, 'Cut, but get ready, she could be here any minute.'

Chris said he was almost out of film and needed another magazine.

'No,' said Carrie, 'she's bound to arrive.'

Chris said, 'It won't take a moment,' and nodded to Carlo, who had another loaded magazine in his hand ready for the change.

Meanwhile, I had checked and found I only had a minute of tape left, so was already changing rolls.

Naturally, a large black Rolls pulled up, and a cry went up, 'It's her – it's Madonna!'

I could tell by Carrie's 'reaction' it most certainly was Madonna, of that there was no doubt, and by the time Chris had got the camera on his shoulder and I had slung the recorder round my neck Madonna was safely inside the ICA.

Carrie's ace team had been found wanting.

Carrie was not best pleased.

Hugh came up to us and said, 'What a waste of time, none of us got a single shot.'

Carrie asked him, 'Why?'

'She got out of the car, and four bodyguards surrounded her, they pushed her head down, hurried her inside and we didn't see a thing – nobody got a shot.'

It was proving not to be a good night.

It was 12:30 a.m. and we were debating whether to call it a day, or 'the next day', as someone said. 'We'll give it half an hour,' said Carrie, and that was thought to be reasonable.

Just before 1 a.m. there was some commotion among the photographers on the steps in front of the statue of the Grand Old Duke of York.

Hugh was already running towards the noise, and Chris, who is always like a coiled spring, was only a few paces behind. The rest did a cavalry charge from the rear with me riding shotgun, and trying to catch up.

When we reached the herd of paparazzi, shutters were being fired in rapid repeat mode, but they weren't shouting for Madonna, they were calling, 'Pamela – this way – Pamela!'

I soon discovered it was Pamela Anderson, the reconstructed *Baywatch* babe wearing what must have been a very cheap frock from the amount of material needed to make it.

After two or three minutes, four large men parted the crowd and collected Miss Anderson, who disappeared into a waiting car.

Hugh explained, 'When they have been hanging around for hours without taking a shot, it only takes one attractive, busty blonde to appear, and there is a sort of feeding frenzy. A couple of hundred pictures are taken within two minutes, and they all know only one or two of them will be used – but who knows, it could just be one of mine.'

Hugh also told us, he had heard that Madonna's Rolls was now at the back of the ICA and he was going to wait there. We joined him.

To this day I don't know how Chris managed to get inside the railings and about ten feet from the Rolls, but he is intrepid, and totally fearless in the face of American Muscle. Always the perpetual optimist – after all, he is a devout Spurs supporter.

Hugh's hunch paid off. Within ten minutes there was some noises and a door opened which Madonna walked through and down the steps to a battery of flashbulbs.

Hugh was wearing a radio mic and I could hear his camera shutter was in overdrive. I saw Chris getting ever closer to the back of the Rolls, and therefore closer to Madonna. A man of such vast proportions (one could only wonder what he had been fed on) was moving towards Chris. In my headphones I heard Hugh give a mighty yell, '*Yes – oh, yesss!*' He had got the shot he was after, and Chris had 'probably' got his.

Carrie smiled and displayed much pleasure. It was 1:30 a.m. so we all went home.

The Kon-Tiki Man and Tigris

The 'beyond belief' phone call came in May 1977 from the BBC. Thor Heyerdahl – The Kon-Tiki Man – the ultimate adventurer – had been a world hero of mine since 1952, when the school took us to a local cinema to see his film of the Kon-Tiki Expedition – a remarkable drift voyage on a balsawood raft, he called *Kon-Tiki* after the Peruvian son of the sun god. The voyage crossed the Pacific Ocean from Peru to an island in Polynesia. It captured my imagination, and I believe the imagination of every kid in the school. This same Thor Heyerdahl, in 1977, was going to build a reed boat in the marshes of Southern Iraq, at the confluence of the river Euphrates and the river Tigris. In fact, right slap bang in the middle of the Garden of Eden, as it was then known.

The BBC *Chronicle* department had been approached to make a documentary on the entire project, which was scheduled to take about three months, and Martin, David and myself were asked if we could work on the film. As it happened, Martin had also been fired up by the *Kon-Tiki* adventure, and David thought it a cracking idea. We were on.

After a short holiday with my wife and children on the Isle of Wight, I left them on August 16th. I picked up a *Daily Mirror* from the seat on the hovercraft travelling from the Isle of Wight to Portsmouth, only to be stunned by the front page: *ELVIS IS DEAD*, with a large picture of 'the King' at full throttle. It's the only precise date related to the start of any job I can remember, because Thor Heyerdahl had chosen the same day to fly us to Iraq.

The Iraqi Airlines 747 taxied out towards the end of the runway at Heathrow, and stopped. After about twenty minutes we were told that there would be a slight delay before take-off due to 'something technical'. The stewardesses flashed stunningly white smiles at us, black/brown eyes shining with a rich warm glow, convincing us that the orange juice they had given us was exactly what we required to take our minds off 'something technical'.

(I'm sure they were called 'stewardesses' then, and not the gender-free 'flight attendant'.)

As it happens we were towards the end of the runway for about three hours before 'something technical' was found to pass muster. Awash with pints of orange juice we finally headed for Baghdad and the Marshes of Southern Iraq.

A month or so earlier we had met Thor Heyerdahl at the University of Southampton where we had taken some film of him with a model of the proposed reed boat. He is immediately likeable, and in a relaxed and friendly manner talked to us about his plans for building the boat. That's always the first hurdle with anyone you have to work with every day for almost three months – how soon will they drive me crazy? How long before I need to commit murder? With Thor I had a good feeling that we would last the course.

It was on this particular day at the university that Thor had mentioned the only thing he could promise us in southern Iraq, in August, was some very unpleasant heat. This wasn't said in a way, which intended to be alarmist, or 'by the way, I expect we might get a slight tan'; it was more a simple statement of fact, which I disregarded at the time.

As we approached Baghdad, at about 10,000 feet, the captain told us in a most pleasant manner that we would be landing in about twenty minutes and that the weather in Baghdad was fine, the local time was 4 a.m. and the temperature was 40° with the humidity at 100% – and he hoped we had enjoyed our flight.

David and I were too bemused by the captain's meteorological mistake to register whether we had enjoyed the flight – I expect that we had, we usually did, David is always good company to travel with, but we were both looking at each other in a state of quandary.

'Look here,' I said, sounding as though I knew something David and the captain could not possibly know, 'It's four in the morning, the man must have said 14° and we just misheard him.' I could tell by David's expression that he wasn't buying that one. 'Well, okay,' I said, 'tell me what you thought he said.'

'I thought he said 40 degrees,' said David.

'How could he have said forty degrees when it's four in the morning?' I said.

'Well, it sounded more like forty than fourteen to me,' he replied.

We were soon inside the baggage reclaim area awaiting the arrival of thirty or so shiny metal boxes along with our personal bags.

Now there are times when David can be downright irritating, and as I stood by the carousel, eagerly bag-spotting, with sweat dripping from all of me, he said with that infuriating smile, 'It would appear that the captain gave us the correct information.' (Apparently the night-time temperature in Baghdad plummets to a nominal 40° in August.) The trouble is David's never smug enough to say that he was right, he qualifies his underlying smugness by complimenting the captain on 'appearing to be right', knowing what the correct temperature would be at 4 a.m. during August.

The following day we were due to meet Thor and do some filming at the Baghdad Museum. Thor felt that the Sumerian scrolls and the cuneiform script lent good evidence to his theory that the cradle of civilisation was indeed in the Gulf, with the Sumerians being competent shipbuilders and also master mariners.

While we waited in the hotel for our man from the Ministry of Information to escort us to the museum, we noticed that about a dozen cars parked outside the hotel all appeared to have caught the same disease. Each one had the bonnet and boot open and a small group of men stood around each vehicle. Some of the men were in Western dress, and some in Arabic dress so it was difficult to identify the owners, the mechanics or simply just passers-by. One thing they all had in common was a unified interest in the engine of each vehicle, but nobody was doing anything. As we were observing this unusual scene two taxis pulled up outside the hotel and from the front taxi came our man from the Ministry; the second taxi was empty, apart from the driver, but was obviously under the control of our man from the Ministry as he was talking to him and gesturing towards the hotel.

It was then that something quite bizarre occurred. No sooner had our man left his car than both cars caught exactly the same disease as the other cars. The bonnet and boot of both vehicles flew open at the same time. We thought, Good grief – when cars catch a virus around Baghdad, it's pretty instant and looks pretty terminal!

The man from the Ministry told us Thor was already at the Museum and we should load up into the two taxis he had waiting for us.

I thought, This is all very well, but hasn't he noticed that since leaving the vehicles, both have gone down with a serious attack of rampant bonnet and boot, which is rapidly reaching epidemic proportions?

I made so bold as to point this out to him, politely of course, he laughed and beckoned us outside to load up. It was only then that we realised the air conditioning in the hotel was so good that the 45° heat outside was impossible to imagine, and any car automatically opened bonnet and boot to avoid it becoming an oven and cooking the engine.

It puzzled us why the taxi drivers decked the back seats of their cars with a thick plastic seat cover, which, in those temperatures became unbearable to sit on. Fortunately our jeans gave us some protection and we arrived at the museum with only lightly grilled buttocks.

The unpleasant heat Thor had mentioned in Southampton was rapidly becoming apparent, so after a couple of days filming clay tablets and impressions of reed boats in the museum with Thor, we were relieved to get on a plane for Basra, which we knew to be a port, where hopefully there could be a light breeze coming off the water.

The last stage of the journey from Basra to the small town of Qurna, where the rivers Tigris and Euphrates meet, took about an hour. I felt pretty excited, if a little apprehensive. After all, it's not every day of the week you get to see Adam's Tree, stay in the Garden of Eden, and put your feet up on Abraham's patch, otherwise known as the cradle of civilisation.

The hotel was called the Garden of Eden Resthouse; it said so over the main door in white tiled lettering on a powerful dark black/blue background. It was built as a single storey at ground floor level spreading some fifty yards either side of the main entrance. The large reception area had a small desk with an Iraqi flag on it. On the wall behind the desk was a picture of Saddam Hussein, and in the corner was a large black and white television playing continuous Iraqi music. Outside the hotel, at the far end were three building-type chaps. I only deduced this as they were surrounded by piles of home-made bricks, some lengths of copper pipe, a couple of 'newish' looking air-conditioning units and a hammer. All three were smoking cigarettes; actually they were continually smoking cigarettes, and none of them were working. The question which came to mind was, 'Does this auger well?'

The hotel couldn't have been better situated for Thor Heyerdahl and his crew, as the grounds went right down to the edge of the River Tigris, and it would be an ideal spot to build and launch the reed boat.

David and Martin decided to check the layout of the hotel while I thought I'd see if I could locate Adam's Tree. In Genesis Chapter 2 we are told that God placed two particular trees in the middle of the garden, one was the tree of life and the other one the tree of knowledge of good and evil. It was this second tree, the fruit of which, God told Adam and Eve they should not eat or touch.

The sign at the side of the road indicated Adam's Tree was a short distance away. I soon came to another sign telling me that I had arrived at Adam's Tree, but all I could see were hundreds and hundreds of palm trees. Not far off, towards the river was a circular wall interspersed with iron railings. As I got closer I saw a sign written in Arabic and in English, which told me that I had found Adam's Tree where Abraham used to pray about 2,000 BC.

The gateway in the wall led to an imprisoned, gnarled, and quite frankly, bent apology for a tree. I was not impressed. The only thing it had going for it was its age, whatever it was; it had to be incredibly old. It was still living, and had some green leaves, even in 47° and 100% humidity. The other curious fact was that it was the only tree of its kind around those parts, the other million or so being palm trees; and it was, as described in Genesis, right at the confluence of the rivers Tigris and Euphrates.

When I got back to the hotel, Martin and David told me about the novel plumbing arrangements they had discovered. The bathrooms and the lavatories had above-floor plumbing with copper pipes travelling approximately four inches above floor level, forming a sort of maze you had to step over to get to the bath or the toilet. The other feature of interest was the lack of air conditioning in any of the bedrooms.

Our sole purpose for being in Southern Iraq during the hottest part of the year was to film Thor having a look at the reeds in the marshes, meeting the Marsh Arabs and organising the cutting of the reeds. Apparently, this is the best time of the year to cut the reeds, as they have absorbed less water, and are therefore much more buoyant. Another advantage of using Qurna as the base to build the boat was its accessibility to the marshes. It only took about ten minutes to drive to the marshes from the Resthouse.

The following morning we left the Garden of Eden about 6:30 a.m. and headed for the marshes. Even at that time of day the temperature was around 42°, and still no hint of that light breeze from the water.

I suppose 'wonder' was my first reaction at seeing the marshes and meeting the Marsh Arabs. It felt as though I had travelled back some four or five thousand years. The marshes cover some six thousand square miles and provide housing, schools and farming for hundreds of Arab families.

We loaded our cases and film gear into three flat-bottomed boats. Cushions had been placed in them for us to sit on, each boat being propelled by a Marsh Arab with a long pole. The reeds were about eight to ten feet tall, having small channels cut through them for the boats to move along. Within a few moments we had turned a bend and the reeds closed in behind us forming a complete screen to the outside world. We were now with a civilisation that has existed here, unchanged, for thousands of years. It felt quite unreal, almost dreamlike.

A few minutes further on we were passing small islands with houses made from the reeds, and some larger buildings made from bundles of reeds. Thor explained to us that it was from bundles similar to these that he would be building his reed boat.

We passed children being taken to school by Arab mums, the only difference from Blighty were the people carriers. Volvo and

Range Rover had no hand in the construction; there were no parking meters or yellow lines. The mums and the children all smiled at us, with our peculiar cargo of metal boxes. It was a peaceful, tranquil atmosphere even if the temperature was climbing to around 48°.

Thor thought we should start filming him inspecting the reeds with some of the Marsh Arabs before the temperature got too unbearable. This sounded like a particularly good idea to me as I was rapidly taking on the appearance of a soggy sponge.

Martin and Thor checked with our interpreter that it was okay to go into the water, and that there was no bilharzia around. We had been warned about the possibility of the disease, caught from a minute worm which lives on a snail shell, and given the chance would burrow through your skin in seconds to multiply rapidly. Death was slow and painful for you, not the worm. Our man from the Ministry of Information assured us that the marshes were clear from bilharzia, and Thor promptly jumped into the water. We had only been filming for a short time when a small shell floated past Thor.

'If you don't have bilharzia then what's this?' said Thor, showing the shell to our man.

'That's not bilharzia – only the house of bilharzia.'

I was amazed how quickly Thor got back into the boat.

By mid-morning we had finished shooting the sequence and Thor gave the okay to the Marsh Arabs to start cutting the reeds. He reckoned it would take three to four weeks to cut and deliver the reeds to the Garden of Eden, by which time the wooden jig in which the boat was to be built should be finished.

My body was beginning to tell me it didn't want to be there any longer. Each of us was now soaking with sweat. This means wet through to our underwear and socks. Even our protective hats were dripping sweat. The humidity was a 100% and the temperature had touched 50° in the shade. The problem was that there was no shade. David noticed that I looked decidedly rancid and had lost my usual Yorkshire sparkle. Now that's what I may have looked like from the outside, but from the inside I was convinced I was about to die. Breathing in that heat was difficult, and every breath felt like someone had pushed a hot wet towel

The Kon-Tiki Man and Tigris

into your mouth. After about fifteen minutes we reached a small reed island where some of our metal boxes had been stored, and I decided that instead of helping Martin and David pack the camera gear away, I would just expire.

I pulled myself out of the boat and into the shade of a reed house where I felt I could pass away with minimum possible fuss. I was aware I could hear voices and mutterings, but nothing intelligible.

I was about to shed my mortal coil, when something quite wonderful happened.

I heard a voice say, 'Drink this, but slowly.'

It was David who crouched by me, with a bottle of clean, cold water in his hand. 'Have a few sips, you'll feel better.'

It was the best drink I have had in my entire life.

How does he do it? We didn't have a fridge, we didn't have cold water, and neither do the Marsh Arabs. How does David always turn up at the right time, with exactly what you need?

It was good to get back to the Garden of Eden, where even Iraqi beer tasted good.

The BBC flew us back to London whilst the reeds were being cut; after all, they couldn't afford to have two lads from Yorkshire and a stripling from Liverpool on the loose in Iraq.

After four weeks we were back in the Garden of Eden, with plenty of lightweight summer clothing and lashings of clean underwear. We were ready for the next two and a half months, no matter what the temperature threw at us.

I was surprised at the speed with which the Marsh Arabs had cut the reeds and the vast quantity stacked in neat long 'haystacks' around the garden area. A young Norwegian, known as HP together with a couple of Iraqi carpenters, had assembled an impressive jig adjacent to the river Tigris, in which the boat would be built. HP was to be a crew member on the voyage, and it appeared to us that with his talent for building wooden jigs, and his obvious dexterity in all matters physical, he was a wise choice to have on board.

The following morning we were surveying the territory from the roof of the hotel and noticed a few men in Western dress with measuring tapes taking readings from the jig to the hotel. They then measured the length of the jig, and the width. It was about this time that Thor arrived on the scene and asked the men what was the purpose of their visit. The men were apparently from the Ministry of Information in Baghdad and were taking measurements to accommodate the new hotel extension. This would increase the hotel capacity by twenty-five bedrooms, Thor told us later.

'The man from the Ministry wants the jig building two metres closer to the road,' said our interpreter.

'Not so,' said Thor, 'we must keep as close to the river as we can.'

The little man from Baghdad smiled politely, and indicated with his arms where he required the jig to be moved.

'The closer to the banks of the river the easier the launching will be,' said Thor.

'*Launching?*' he said, 'did you say, *launching?*'

'Of course,' said Thor smiling. 'You don't expect me to leave the ship on the shore?'

'Ship?' The man from Ministry looked puzzled; all he could see were piles upon piles of straw.

His expression told us he thought Thor had recently escaped from some asylum.

'You can call it a haystack if you like, but to me it will always be a ship,' said Thor.

The little man half smiled and said, 'Now you make fun of me. I'm sorry, sir, but I have orders from the Ministry of Information.'

'That must be the same Ministry that has given me permission in writing to build my ship here,' replied Thor.

'Sir, I have the masons and carpenters ready to start tomorrow, we have to add twenty-five rooms to the Resthouse,' he said, pointing to the area by the jig.

It became obvious that this was one department in the Ministry of Information not speaking to the other department in the Ministry.

'If you build your extension now, I cannot build my ship. But if I build my ship now, where I planned, we will sail away in two months, and you can begin building your hotel extension.'

The little man from the Ministry nodded, smiled, complied and with a gesture indicated he was a dead man in Baghdad.

One of the first things always to be done, on any lengthy location such as this, is to sort out money and transport. We had a BBC *Chronicle* producer with us, Bruce Norman, an experienced and likeable man who had been given a plain envelope with 'Trav Cheques' written on it. Bruce had been given the envelope only a few hours before he got on the plane, and opened it on the flight to find the BBC had covered all eventualities with their usual care. The £5,000 pounds in Barclays Bank traveller's cheques would certainly cover us for the first three weeks until the American director, Dale Bell, from *National Geographic* arrived.

Bruce headed for Basra and a large bank.

We began filming Thor and the Marsh Arabs, who were now forming the reeds into 70-foot long bundles to begin the assembly of the boat. We soon realised that one bundle was pretty much the same as the next, and as there would be 40 to 50 bundles needed we decided to cover only every tenth or twelfth. This saved on film stock, gave the boat more time to take shape, and gave us time to become acclimatised to the heat, which fortunately had dropped to a bearable 30°. We could also explore the town of Qurna, and meet a few of the key characters.

This appealed to David, as he was always keen to meet key characters in any part of the world.

Bruce returned from his trip to Basra with an expression that did not bode well. He immediately called us to our room for a chat. I say our room, because this time five of us were sharing one large room. The bonus of this room was that the three building-type chaps we had observed on our previous visit had recently fitted an air conditioner. We deduced it must be them, as we hadn't seen any other builders around besides the Marsh Arabs, and their speciality was reeds, not air conditioning. It was good to have a room with an air conditioner even if it had a two-inch gap around it to the outside world and the outside heat. David disappeared and soon returned with some towels. He made the intrepid journey hurdling the pipes in the bathroom, soaked the towels in water and jammed them into the gap around the unit making it as airtight as possible, and as usual – it worked.

It soon became apparent to us that practically all men in Iraq smoke cigarettes, and in large quantities. If any hostile country wished to overthrow Iraq it would cost very little. A total embargo on all cigarette sales to Iraq, from anywhere in the world, would have the male population gibbering psychotics within a week or so.

I think I could be accused of digressing – Bruce had just got back from the bank in Basra.

Unlike me, Bruce came straight to the point. The Barclays Bank traveller's cheques given to Bruce by the BBC could not be cashed anywhere in Iraq, as Barclays Bank was one of the major banks supporting Israel in the war of 1967. We had no money.

Just when things look a trifle bleak, the unexpected comes round the corner. A couple of minutes walk from the Garden of Eden was what I believe the Iraqis called, a 'gentleman's club' that served Iraqi beer. Now as we didn't have any Iraqi money, all except David, we couldn't buy any Iraqi beer, so how come we were sitting in the 'gentleman's club' drinking five Iraqi beers? Quite probably, the Mayor of Qurna had made some deal with the manager of our hotel, whose brother ran the 'gentleman's club'. The word on the street was that we must be 'loaded' or at least pretty well-heeled. After all, we had come all the way from London, and the BBC had to be 'reckoned with' as having considerable clout, plus there were about to arrive at the hotel, more of the species, from the USA – Japan – Russia – Scandinavia – Mexico – and Italy. That's a whole mountain of dollars about to come through the door. We were 'on tick' until the cavalry arrived, and anyway, the manager of the hotel had our passports in his safe – we were not going anywhere.

Four Aymara Indians arrived from Bolivia, to oversee the building of the boat. These were the same people Thor used to help him build his papyrus-ship, *Ra II*. The men from Lake Titicaca knew about reed boats, plus anything you knew about reeds, and cared throw at them. They were impressed by the Marsh Arabs, and their building technique using reed bundles. They told Thor that the Marsh Arabs were far superior to the Arabs of North Africa. As was to be proven later. This became a good all-round working relationship.

Most days we would work from 6:30 a.m. to 10-ish when it was cooler, and then in the late afternoon. This gave us three to four hours a day to 'do our own thing'. Most of us would read, listen to some music, write home in hope that the letter would arrive before we got back, and it gave David time to make 'arrangements' with whoever regarding whatever.

Being of a devious nature, I found a quiet spot on the flat roof of the hotel, shaded by some date palms, and shielded from the noise of the town. Quiet mattered, as I enjoy music, and had brought with me some audio cassettes. Either the others didn't know where I was or they were very kind in not disturbing me – all except for Martin, who would give me a yell if we were about to go into action with Thor. I suppose one major deterrent could have been the type of music I was playing, Prokofiev and Martinu are not classed as easy listening in HMV, and I would always try not to inflict either of them on friends. One sure-fire way of spreading a bout of 'expedition fever', as Thor called it, was hearing the same tune day in, day out, or someone just whistling non-stop when you can't get away from it. So prolonged Shostakovich or Copland wasn't going to help anybody, except for the devious one on the roof.

Over the next couple of weeks we filmed bundles ten and twelve being finished and put in place. During this time other members of Thor's crew began to arrive. They altered the whole character of the Garden of Eden. Norman Baker from the USA; Yuri Senkevich, a doctor and TV presenter from the Soviet Union; and Carlo Mauri, a mountaineer from Italy. These men had all sailed with Thor on his previous two expeditions with *Ra I* and *Ra II,* so there was much greeting, hugging and reminiscing. It was good to have new people around, with new stories, and in particular, new jokes.

During our stay in the Garden of Eden so far, we had only seen, heard or smelled one half of God's creation. We had seen many black shapes moving around the town, and rumour had it that under the 'black shape' was a woman. Well, maybe, but these shapes didn't look anything like women to me.

Giles took it upon himself to put me straight. (I haven't mentioned Giles before – that's very remiss of me). Giles was the fifth member of our crew, who was there 'to lend a hand and be of good cheer'. We had decided back in London that it would sensible for us to have a good all-rounder to help us with whatever. Giles is a professional hot air balloon pilot, and as David called him 'a fine chap and jolly good egg' he seemed to be the obvious choice. The 'black shapes' were supposed to look like that, Giles informed me – it was the Arab custom. It's supposed to stop people like me getting any ideas and becoming decidedly rampant. I was grateful to Giles and promised him I would attempt not to do anything untoward.

We were totally unaware that the other half of God's creation in Eden had already arrived. Mrs Yuri Senkevich, a very attractive blonde lady in her mid-thirties from Moscow, had travelled with her husband, the doctor. Not only did Yuri Senkevich speak good English, his wife spoke immaculate English. She worked in the diplomatic circles of Moscow and of necessity, was required to speak many languages perfectly.

Dr Senkevich introduced his wife, Ksenja, to each of us, and we each, in turn, went all unnecessary and manly – as portrayed by our body language.

At the same time Dale Bell, the director from *National Geographic* arrived, and with him came thousands of US dollars. We were no longer naked in Eden, but had the funds to set up a proper production. It took three to four days to acquire all the facilities to make us fully operational – consequently, it was time for me to get back on the roof.

A couple of mornings later I was in my usual shady spot on the roof when I heard footsteps close by. The music I was playing had just finished, so the footsteps were quite clear.

Mrs Senkevich walked by, wearing a towelling bathrobe. She saw me, said, 'Hello,' smiled and walked on. I said, 'Good morning,' forgot to smile, and picked up my book.

I was playing a Prokofiev piano concerto when I noticed Mrs Senkevich was sunbathing within my eye line, and not out of sight. I wasn't aware she had moved. When the cassette finished she put on her bathrobe, walked towards me, thanked me for the music, smiled and left.

I thought, What a nice lady.

The Kon-Tiki Man and Tigris

The Bolivian Indians, while doing a thorough job with the Marsh Arabs, were not enjoying the heat, as they live at about 12,000 feet in the Andes and the mountains around them are snow capped most of the year. Two of them had gone down with bad sore throats, so Martin mentioned to Thor that I had a medical kit, and probably had something to sort them out. It's true, I did have a medical kit, made up for me by my father-in-law who was a doctor and had access to all we could need. This was the standard kit made up for us since our first trip to Africa, and had covered all eventualities so far.

Bolivian Indians… sore throats… No worries, I thought.

'Doctor Luther K Desmond' set up his clinic near the boat and prepared to administer the medicine. All I had was a bottle of TCP but I thought, This will have to do. I mixed up a moderate solution of TCP (20% TCP, 80% water) and offered it to the Bolivians. They looked at me with total amazement. Do we rub it on something? they enquired, and I realised that we had a communication problem. I took a glass of the solution, poured it into my mouth, gargled then spat it out. I looked at the Indians, about to say, 'That's what you do,' when it was explained to me that the Indians didn't know what I had done. They thought this was some preparation for a ritual yet to come. A translator tried to explain that if they did what I had done, they would be cured of the sore throat. It suddenly dawned on me that we had to teach the Bolivians how to gargle.

After many attempts and much laughter, they thought they had got it. We laughed again, hugged and I declared the clinic was closed.

The following day the Indians returned asking for the same treatment, and I thought the least I can do is to oblige, so this I did. Thor approved of this action, as it kept the Indians working.

What we didn't expect was the rapture the next day when the sore throats had disappeared, and I was declared some kind of medicine man.

There was not much happening the following day, bundles were being bundled, the Bolivian Indians were breathing and swallowing comfortably, Thor was expecting dhow sailors from India, and I thought this is a good time for some Shostakovich.

One can only go so long without musical angst, and this seemed an opportune moment to rectify that situation.

I settled myself in my patch on the roof with cassettes and a book. I had only been there some fifteen minutes before Mrs Senkevich arrived, and with a cheery 'Hello' settled down about ten feet away. There was no need for conversation as Shostakovich was doing it all. I don't know how many of you are familiar with the Tenth Symphony, but I do recommend you try it on for size.

Mrs Senkevich obviously new it well, and felt it to be perfect music whilst getting a suntan. She was now wearing a two-piece, pre-glasnost, light green swimsuit, and absorbing the sun.

I thought, What a lovely lady.

The news had got out about my medical powers and Arabs from the town were forming a queue for me to cure their ailments. It took me about three days to realise that my patients didn't have any problems, they were just curious to see what I had in my medical kit. As I had been treating all the severe headache problems with Paracetamol, David pointed out to me that these people don't have headaches; they just want to be near the boat, and Thor. Give them something else; we may need the Paracetamol ourselves in time. He was right. So for the next few days my patients went away with anti-malarial pills for their problems, and all appeared to be cured.

All was going well for a few days until a mother brought her son to me at the afternoon clinic. He had a large swollen area on his leg and ankle, which appeared to be full of pus. I thought that all I could do was to lance the infected area, treat it with disinfectant, and give him some broad-spectrum antibiotics I had in the medical kit. There must have been a dozen or so 'patients' standing around awaiting treatment. The only sharp knife was in my tool kit, which David promptly fetched. I opened the tool kit, which displayed pliers, wire cutters, a number of screwdrivers and some clamps, which on first glance looked like instruments of torture. Two or three of the 'patients' decided to leave the queue. I found the Stanley knife and disinfected the blade. This, unexpectedly seemed to be a good cure for Iraqi headaches, and more prospective patients left.

I asked the mother, via an Iraqi schoolteacher who had volunteered to be my go-between, to tell the boy that I had to cut the swelling to release the poison. Everyone nodded their approval, even the boy. As quickly as I could I lanced the swollen area, and was immediately showered by pus, as were his mother and two or three bystanders. I cleaned the wound, after removing as much pus as possible, dressed it, and told the mother to give him the antibiotics for a week. She thanked me, and my eyes welled with tears, as I realised I simply didn't have a clue about what I had just done. I looked up for the next patient... everyone had gone.

'I didn't know you were a doctor, I thought you recorded the sound,' said Mrs Senkevich later.

'I'm not a doctor,' I replied. 'I just carry the crew medical kit, which can cause people to jump to conclusions.'

'Whatever you are, you appear to make your patients comfortable,' she said, 'and you have a nice reed side manner.' She smiled. 'What are you reading?'

'It's C S Lewis,' I replied.

'How wonderful,' said Mrs Senkevich. 'We can't buy his books in Russia. Could I have a look at one?'

I offered her the one I was reading; she took the book, and sat down a short distance from me.

Martin called, and we were off to do an update with Thor on the boat.

A couple of days later, the Iraqi schoolteacher, who, fortunately for me spoke excellent English, told me that the boy whose leg I had treated was now walking on it, and with very little pain. I asked the teacher why hadn't the boy gone to the hospital in Basra for treatment. He said that the clinic by the boat was much quicker and was free. The teacher then asked me where I had received my medical training – was it in London? He had, after all, seen inside the medical kit, which contained among other things, hypodermics, morphine and sutures. I told him that I had received a crash course in London on jamming needles into people's bottoms from my father-in-law, and for some reason, which I never discovered, this appeared to satisfy him. What I hadn't realised was the hole I was digging for myself.

That evening the Russian, Doctor Senkevich, approached me, and said that he would like a word with me, away from the others. My first thought, as I left the dining area with him was, Oh 'eck! The doctor was a perfectly formed male in his early forties, whose firm, suntanned legs looked good in his shorts, and his well-muscled arms would have done any middle-weight boxer proud. If things were going to turn ugly, I would have advised anyone to put their money on the doctor. He had an engaging smile, which only served to fuel my anxious state. By now we were outside on a balcony overlooking the River Tigris, and the silhouette of the boat could just be made out with the date palms.

'This will do here,' he said.

'It looks quite adequate to me,' I think I muttered.

'My wife tells me that you have been talking with her on the roof, and playing music,' said the doctor with that smile again.

'I did happen to see her on the roof during some Shostakovich,' I replied inanely.

'Do you intend to carry on reading and playing music on the roof?' he said thoughtfully.

'Well, I could always move to a different place on the roof, if it is disturbing your wife, and her sunbathing.'

'No, no, it is good that you talk with my wife and play music,' said the doctor. 'While I am working with Thor and the others in the day I have no time to see her and I do not wish her to become bored. Please can you play the music on the roof with my wife, when you are not working?'

I thought, Mrs Senkevich is a most attractive lady, and in her pre-glasnost two-piece looked very fetching, and the doctors offer was kind and innocent... It seemed only polite to be of assistance. Red lights were going on in my head, which said 'Eggshells, Desmond, eggshells, tread very carefully'.

I assured Dr Senkevich that I had plenty of music and reading matter left, which I would be more than pleased to share with his wife, on the roof.

When I got back to the others, Giles said to me, 'What was all that about?'

'The Russian doctor would like me to play nice music on the roof, with his wife whenever I am able,' I said.

The Kon-Tiki Man and Tigris

'That sounds decidedly "untoward" if you ask me,' said Giles, 'and you did promise you wouldn't.'

Thor Heyerdahl was pleased with the progress being made on the construction of the boat, and the good atmosphere shared by all nationalities involved. It was anticipated that it would be about two weeks to the launch, providing that the dhow sailors from Bombay arrived to advise Thor about any expected difficulties he might encounter, when taking a reed boat into the Gulf.

The daily clinic was running smoothly, with almost any ailment being cured by a regular dose of anti-malarial pills. In fact, as a medic (albeit 'a bit dodgy') and a musicologist to the USSR (most certainly dodgy) I was 'the business'.

By now the heat had dropped to a modest 25° in the day and a comfortable 15° at night. So it was decided this would be a good time for us to visit Ur of the Chaldeans, the birthplace of Abraham, and the very cradle of civilisation. While there we could also see Erech, a city mentioned in Genesis Chapter 5, not far from Ur. Now this is travelling back in history, to almost the very beginning. For me it didn't get much better.

Having driven around the marshes for some seven hours we got to Ur, only to find signs had been placed on two sides of the ziggurat stating quite simply 'NO PHOTOGRAPH' and we assumed the Arabic markings above read the same warning. The entire area had been sealed off by the Iraqi military. We got back in the vehicle and headed for our accommodation for the night. This proved to be a similar arrangement to that at the Garden of Eden Resthouse; all of us would share one room.

Awakening in the morning, we all quickly discovered it had been a different night from the Garden of Eden. Anything that could fly and had teeth had bitten us. Not once, or twice, but many times. Later, six very lumpy, blotchy, and itchy people got into the minibus and headed back to Qurna. We bounced around on a hot, sweaty bus examining our itching red lumps, and trying desperately not to scratch.

Giles looked at me, grimaced and said, 'I'll be glad when I've had enough of this.'

We were not happy.

The Kon-Tiki Man and Tigris

As we arrived at the Resthouse, so did the dhow sailors from India. It was now almost dark and it was decided the sailors should get some rest and look at the reed boat in the morning.

Mrs Senkevich saw the state of our blotchy, lumpy bodies, and offered us some of her husband's cream for insect bites. She insisted it was very good and had been designed for skin infections and insect bites encountered by the USSR military. The potion was wonderful; within minutes the itching had eased and by morning the blotchy lumps were less inflamed. After another day of treatment with the Soviet wonder cream we were a lot more comfortable. Giles came to me and said, 'You should spend more time on the roof, the Shostakovich is obviously working.'

When I got up the following day, the dhow sailors were already walking around the boat with Thor. Having had the construction of the boat explained to them, and how many would be on the crew, they checked on what type of sails would be used, and asked where the engine would be fitted. Thor looked surprised at their question regarding the engine, and told them that there wouldn't be an engine; this was to be a voyage such as the Sumerians would have taken, using only sails. The dhow sailors looked at each other, and then at Thor, and then at each other again.

'We can be of no help to you,' said a dhow sailor. 'All our boats have engines, we couldn't sail in the Gulf without an engine.'

Thor looked somewhere, the dhow sailors looked at each other again, Thor looked puzzled. It appeared that there had been a rather huge communication problem between some powers somewhere, the BBC, and the maritime authority in India. The three dhow sailors packed quickly, and were soon on their way back to Baghdad and on to Bombay. Very little was heard of them after that.

That afternoon, the schoolteacher told me he had brought a very special case for me to look at. He said that the word had gone around that there was a man by the boat who could heal anything. This same man had operated on a boy who couldn't walk, and within three days the boy was walking, and was now completely cured. I told him that was a special case where I only had to treat the infection. He said he realised that was the case, but a friend of his had a son with damaged legs, which the mother knew I could repair. I said, 'Bring him to me and I'll do whatever's possible.'

After I'd treated with anti-malarial pills some Arabs who were suffering from 'terrible headaches', the schoolteacher brought the mother and her son to me. The only difference was that the boy was being pulled on a trolley because he really couldn't walk. He couldn't walk because his legs were deformed, possibly from birth. I looked at the schoolteacher, mainly out of desperation, and asked him how long the boy had been like this. He told me he had known the boy to be like this since he met the family. I think it was about this time I felt tears of futility welling up. I could do nothing for this child, despite the look of anticipation on the mother's face. She had heard about my wonderful curing powers; I simply handed out anti-malarial pills to Arabs with headaches. This child, who travelled his world with deformed legs buckled under him, on a board attached to roller skates, pulled around by his mother, needed a miracle. My box of hypodermics and bandages had nothing to help him.

The teacher said to me, 'If there is nothing you can do, I will explain to the mother.'

I went to our room, sat on my bed and wept like a child.

The day of the launch followed three days of torrential rain. Thor was concerned that the bundles of reeds would have soaked up too much water before the boat was even in the river. The news of the launch date had spread much further than any of us could have anticipated, and by the afternoon hundreds of people had arrived at the Garden of Eden. The Marsh Arabs were naturally there in force, with their families. The large Mayor of Qurna, and his necessary retinue were forthcoming and doing what a mayor and retinue do on such occasions. Dignitaries from the Ministry in Baghdad arrived in suits, and proudly displayed a white ribbon, and a pair of scissors, which had been purchased specially in Baghdad, for the Director General of the Ministry, no less, to cut the ribbon in a proper ceremony in front of the boat. Thor and his crew buzzed with anticipation; well, the crew buzzed and

The Kon-Tiki Man and Tigris

Thor strode around with authority and command – not all that much of a buzz, actually.

Mrs Senkevich just looked lovely.

The daughter of the head Marsh Arab was to name the boat *Tigris* after six sheep had been sacrificed and their blood rubbed on to the twin bows of the boat. Thor felt that six sheep was a bit excessive and was sure that one would do the job just as well. After some debate it was agreed that one sheep would be sacrificed at the launch, and the other five would be terminated elsewhere, away from the cameras.

Thor made a speech, thanking the Marsh Arabs, his crew, the men from the Ministry in Baghdad, and all who had been part of the boat-building team. The man from the Ministry cut the white ribbon (specially purchased in Baghdad). The head Marsh Arab made a speech, which only the Marsh Arabs could understand, while we just nodded and smiled. The Marsh Arabs sacrificed the sheep and placed handprints of blood on the bow. The daughter named the boat *Tigris* or that is what we think she did.

The boat started to move very slowly down the grease-laden metal tracks it had been built on. The crowd cheered enthusiastically, the large mayor and his retinue made gestures of pleasure, mingled with pride and the men from the Ministry looked very smart and appropriate. The bow of the boat reached the rivers bank and slid into the water. Another mighty cheer went up from the crowd, a loud clap of thunder was heard in the distance, and then the boat stopped.

The metal tracks the boat was sliding along had buckled, and the 60-foot boat was now stuck with its bow in the water and its stern in the air.

People attempted to push the boat as best they could, but to no avail; *Tigris* was a very big and heavy bundle of reeds. There was another loud clap of thunder.

The men in suits took their ribbon and scissors and headed back to Baghdad. The mayor and retinue moved off, and the spectators slowly went home.

In the past, David's timing has usually been precise, well gauged, and appropriate. The previous night David had a dream, and for reasons only known to himself, David believed that the dream had a direct bearing on the present situation, and felt it incumbent upon him to share the dream with Thor.

I never discovered why, but for some reason Thor always referred to David as 'the young Jewish camera assistant' on the crew. As far as I knew, David couldn't read Hebrew, had not had a barmitz-vah, and was not circumcised on the eighth day.

So as Thor recalled later 'the young Jewish camera assistant' was telling him about a dream he had, which he thought would bring some comfort to Thor at this particular moment. David had dreamt that he saw a vast herd of sheep come on board the boat and devour it, as revenge for their sacrificed friends.

The timing of the telling can only be described as ill timed.

Not long after, Thor heard that the Marsh Arabs had their own ideas for the unsuccessful launch. Not only should they have sacrificed the six sheep, but a bull as well, for a boat that large.

We were wandering about the site, trying to look informed, though of what we knew not. I bent down and picked up short length of reed, and walked towards the boat looking thoughtful, if a little inane, as only men can do in such situations. Giles wanted to know what I was going to do with three foot of reed – perform some Sumerian reed dance and propel the boat into the river? I pondered, put the reed on the ground, and attempted to look even more thoughtful.

'What that needs is a good shove,' said Giles. At least his pondering had come up with a useful conclusion.

My pondering told me it was time to get some food and a Carlsberg. Giles thought this was a good ponder, so we did.

We were probably on our second Carlsberg when someone shouted, 'The Russians are here, where's Yuri?'

Sure enough the Russians were here, two of them, big chaps with a very big truck. Yuri explained to them what the problem was, and suddenly reed matting was rolled up and fixed to the truck.

Gently, the monster vehicle moved forward and the boat began to ease into the river.

'I said it needed a good shove,' said Giles, 'and that's what I call a good shove... must be forty to fifty tons of truck there.'

The following morning I was on the balcony about 6 a.m.

The Kon-Tiki Man and Tigris

looking at the boat with a certain amount of wonder. There was this twin-hulled reed boat floating perfectly, and looking simply beautiful in the low early morning sun.

In August we had filmed the reeds being cut by the Marsh Arabs, and Thor's dream had begun. It was now the middle of November and his boat was floating on the River Tigris as forecast. He was right on schedule.

I couldn't help thinking, It took a man of vision, remarkable planning, and a whole lot of nerve to pull this off.

Within days, the cabins, the 'A' frame mast, sails and twin rudders plus 'the usual offices' had been added. Stores and provisions were loaded, and *Tigris* was ready to leave the Garden of Eden.

When *Tigris*, with Thor and crew left the Garden of Eden, we found it a far more moving experience than had been anticipated. There were wet eyes everywhere, real men with muscles, standing with legs apart, could be seen to shed a tear.

Next day we packed, and left the Garden of Eden Resthouse, the Tigris and Euphrates, Adam's Tree, the large mayor, and Mrs Senkevich.

I had given Mrs Senkevich all the C S Lewis books I had, plus a couple of others. She held my hand, kissed me on the cheek, and said, 'Goodbye... thank you for sharing your music.'

I thought, Mrs Senkevich, you are a lovely lady.

She was heading north for Baghdad and Moscow. We were going south to Basra for one night and then flying on to Bahrain.

Dale Bell told us that our hotel in Basra would have telephones and telegram facilities, so we could phone home, and also cable the BBC for luxuries in Bahrain.

The hotel did indeed have telephones, but the lines from Basra to London were as stable as a chocolate teapot.

Dale was to contact the BBC by cable later that evening, so we decided he could give them our personal requests for Bahrain.

I should have mentioned before that the Garden of Eden restaurant at the Resthouse seemed only to specialise in either chicken, pieces of chicken, or shredded chicken with a side salad of tomatoes. You could have the chicken well done and dripping in fat, in fact so well done it was dark brown and the size of a

The Kon-Tiki Man and Tigris

healthy sparrow, or you could have the chicken pieces, or shredded chicken cold, or incredibly cold, depending on the setting of the fridge and random power cuts. Or there was 'Sli-Sli', which incorporated slices of beef with a side salad of tomatoes. This you could only have cold, or incredibly cold, depending on the fridge and power cuts.

Variations of the above were reasonably safe, and only one of us got salmonella poisoning.

There were other Iraqi dishes, which some did try, but the percentage of those going down with 'Bombay Belly' and 'Poona Crut' was too high to risk, so most of us stuck to beef or chicken.

With this fresh in our memories, we plotted our requests to the BBC.

I think most of us asked for clean sheets, a bathroom with normal plumbing, a fillet steak, clean drinking water, tablecloths, friendly air conditioning, a room with a view, and I know I asked for a Banana Split with lashings of ice cream. These were the sort of requests we all felt were in the power of the BBC to grant, and wouldn't blow their budget.

All of us, that is except for David, who had a very functional demand. His telegram simply said, 'SEND MORE SHEEP'

We never did hear how this was received by the BBC.

We flew from Basra to Baghdad, and then on to Bahrain to await the arrival of Thor and his crew.

The Gulf Hotel was magnificent, and at first we thought a terrible mistake had been made. We knew we would soon be moved to a hotel more befitting our station, but not so – this was it.

My room on the seventh floor had a view overlooking the sea, a bowl of fresh fruit with a note to me by name, not just 'We welcome you to...' but 'Welcome Mr Desmond to the Gulf Hotel we trust...' And it was printed, not written by hand. I thought, Now there's posh. The double bed was so vast it went into perspective, and it felt as though it took at least a couple of minutes to walk to the bathroom, and this was all for me, all mine.

That evening we showered and polished ourselves for the first time in almost three months, and had dinner in the most luxurious restaurant in the hotel.

The intrepid trio - Martin, David and KD
at Shepperton Studios (c.1975)

Shangilla minder - Lake Rudolf, Kenya
'Do not mess with me - sunshine'
David Graham

The Shangilla press club arrive - Lake Rudolf, Kenya
1974
David Graham

David's photographic duel with Shangilla
cameraman of the year
KD

Carroll Baker at the time of 'The Carpetbaggers'

David, Peter and KD leaving Johannesburg in the
getaway vehicle - Lesotho 1975
David Graham

David and teeth - photo taken by me - Lesotho 1975
KD

Me plus designer hat - Lesotho 1975
David Graham

Bath time for David at 10,000 feet - Lesotho 1975
KD

Local 'Pan's People' turn up - Lesotho 1975
David Graham

'Pan's People' about to rumble - Lesotho 1975
David Graham

Martin filming some cool dudes at the party
Lesotho 1975
David Graham

Dancers at the Christmas Do - Lesotho 1975
David Graham

Schoolgirls check me out - Lesotho 1975
David Graham

Masai hitching a ride in the balloon - Kenya 1976
David Graham

A few Masai make it into the basket - Kenya 1976
David Graham

An aardvark called 'Million' - Kenya 1976
David Graham

The 6.30am flight at Amboseli Game Reserve
Kenya 1976
David Graham

'A Bridge Too Far' - Holland 1976
'What did you do in the war Daddy?'
David Graham

Iain Johnstone interviews Dirk Bogarde in Holland on
'A Bridge Too Far' (c.1976) *David Graham*

Martin filming Thor Heyerdahl working with
the marsh Arabs - Iraq 1976 *David Graham*

Thor Heyerdahl checks construction of his reed boat
'Tigris' - Southern Iraq 1976
David Graham

Mrs Senkevich and me - in the Garden of Eden
Southern Iraq 1976
David Graham

'Tigris' sails down the Shatt al Arab to Basra - Iraq 1976
David Graham

Thor Heyerdahl and his crew navigate the waters of Southern Iraq and head for the Arabian Gulf
David Graham

Ursula Andress as Aphrodite - such as memory goes

Martin and me with 'Mother Russia'
Volgograd, Russia 1987
Mary-Ellen Mark

Alan Root filming Kopjes in Tanzania - 1990 *David Graham*

Censorship only required to protect the
innocent and my mother - UK 1994

Catching up with the paperwork whilst heaving
and rolling on the high seas (c.1995)
Michael Proudfoot

Cunningly disguised, and totally unrecognisable we
avoid detection - UK 1994
Carrie Britton

Sharing a close moment with Jeremy over breakfast
New York (c.1999)

Emma with furry friends, Chris (the cameraman)
and KD on location with the Manchester Police
Jeremy Llewellyn-Jones

Me with technical spaghetti of my own making on
'Jonathan Millers - Operaworks' (c.1996)
Henrietta Butler

David with teeth and Harry
(c.2002)

Needless to say, there were tablecloths, very clean white tablecloths, clean knives and forks, clean drinking water with ice, and white napkins that cracked when opened.

I remember we had steaks and fresh vegetables, and I did have a gloriously huge banana split for pud.

We had a wonderful, if somewhat dreamlike, time. Did I mention that we also had bottles of wine? That night most of us were very ill; our bodies just couldn't cope with the rich food.

The next ten days were spent in the total lap of luxury. I had never known before where this lap was; I had heard rumours, but now I knew for sure. It was at the Gulf Hotel in Bahrain, sunbathing by the pool, with chaps in white jackets and black trousers bringing drinks of one's choice to one's poolside table. David requesting more ice please, Giles and myself going through the routine of playing tennis, and saying, 'Well, yah, splendid shot,' long before 'yuppies' had been invented; and then being persuaded to rest by the pool, where chaps in white jackets and black trousers would bring us more drinks, before our buttocks had time to settle on well-padded recliners.

Call us foolhardy, but we felt this was a lifestyle to which one could easily become accustomed. There was even a slim chance we could become 'gentlemen'.

I did suggest you call us foolhardy.

After ten days of living way beyond the means of the BBC, and still no sight of Thor, or his boat, the BBC decided to call us back to London.

This did make sense, as it was now early December, and the last they had heard from the boat was news it was moored on Failaka Island, a long way north of Bahrain.

We packed our considerable gear, and flew back to London the following day, much to the surprise and relief of our families.

The next day, David called and asked if I could be ready to fly back to Bahrain in the morning, as *Tigris* was being towed by a Russian ship, and should be in Bahrain in a couple of days.

My wife, who was used to the vagaries of our industry, smiled and asked if I thought I'd be home for Christmas, I assured her, as men do in such circumstances, that of course I'd be back in time for Christmas.

David, Giles and myself (minus Martin, who had work booked elsewhere) flew back to Bahrain, which hadn't changed much since our last visit. The bar staff at the Gulf Hotel were delighted we had returned, as were the crew of the *Tigris*, the arrival of which we had missed by a day.

It never ceases to surprise me, that we allegedly earn our living by the communicating to the world, and yet we have great difficulty in communicating with each other.

While Thor was having alternative sails made for the boat, and attending functions of considerable meaning in Bahrain, we found ourselves forced 'poolside' once more.

After a couple of weeks of this unexpected yet pleasing sort of treatment, interspersed by a bit of filming at various archaeological sites, accompanied by the random interview, we packed our bags again, and said farewell to Thor and his crew.

On December 22nd we arrived back in London, and just made it under the wire for Christmas.

★

After five months at sea and 4,200 miles of remarkable navigation, the *Tigris* was forced to terminate its journey due to the war in the Gulf of Aden. The small Republic of Djibouti alone allowed Thor and the crew access. Warships surrounded the entrance to the Gulf, and it rapidly became evident that it would be impossible to take on supplies, as everything was geared to the war effort.

The crew of *Tigris* wrote a letter to Kurt Waldheim, the Secretary-General of the United Nations, expressing their dismay and sorrow at the conflict surrounding them, and that evening at sunset, as a token gesture against all wars, Thor and his men set fire to the *Tigris*.

Jairus Jiri – Zimbabwe

I was surprised to get a phone call in November 1981 from a cameraman I had never worked with before asking me if I would like to work with him in Zimbabwe for three weeks on a project relating to children who had survived the civil war in that country. Our brief would be to follow a man called Jairus Jiri, a local benefactor, who had set up special schools and dormitories for the children in most of the major towns in Zimbabwe.

In mid-November five of us flew to Harare, but when we got to the hotel we were asked if we could share rooms as it would help the budget. Normally, I would never share a room (except with David and his teeth), this is usually the only space you have to call your own and to get away from the rest of the crew. Three weeks of sharing the same space with a crew can develop claustrophobia to a point where 'murder' seems the only reasonable option. However, on this occasion I was more than a little fortunate. The good Lord had smiled on me and had brought along with us a Dutch assistant film editor who was there to lend a hand, as he was in between films and had never been to Zimbabwe. I had chatted to him on the journey and found him to be most pleasant so before anyone else snapped him up I said, 'I'll share with Stuart, if he has no objection.' He hadn't, so we shared, and a friendship began which has lasted for more than twenty years.

The following day we met Jairus Jiri. He was not at all how I had expected him to be. He was tall, large, with a lovely gentle smile and the warmth of an inner peace that was hard to describe. This man displayed integrity wherever he went without apparently having to do anything. He was a retired shopkeeper who had sold his shop and raised money for the children injured in the civil war. Schools with sleeping accommodation had been bought or built and, with some help from the government, these places had been staffed with special needs teachers, doctors and health workers to care for the children. It still hadn't dawned on

Jairus Jiri – Zimbabwe

me that these children were either blind, limbless, deaf or a combination of all three.

Not knowing quite what to expect the following day, we travelled to the first school just outside Harare. The staff welcomed us warmly and told us the children would be pleased to let us watch them dancing and singing.

We arrived at an area outside a classroom where the children had already started to sing and dance – and with such enthusiasm it was infectious. The group dancing had seed pods tied to their ankles and wrists which had the effect of orchestrated rattles that drove the rhythm along with great energy. I was looking at the group of children who appeared to be about nine to twelve year olds, but could not see any signs of war damage. Their smiles were the most wonderful I had yet to see – they simply radiated happiness – they danced and sang and smiled. Perhaps it was that they all had the most perfectly white teeth; they certainly had remarkable teeth by any standard, and even David, had he been there, would have been reluctant to smile at full throttle. Most African children have cleaned their teeth with bits of twig since they first had teeth – and with great success; perhaps the Western world has yet to learn.

These children, however, were not displaying their skills in dental twigmanship; they were, without any debate, showing a total freedom of spirit and happiness. We were each puzzled as to why they should feel this way, after all many were blind, a lot of them were deaf and some maimed from stepping on landmines. All of them had lost their parents.

When questioned later, Jairus Jiri explained to us his deep Christian faith, and told us of the love God had shown him in his life. He added that the price Jesus had paid on the cross to purchase a Zimbabwe shopkeeper for eternity was unconditional love beyond all understanding, and all he was trying to do was to show these children a part of this love in some way. His sole desire was to praise God and to thank Him for all he had been given. Jairus Jiri felt that in showing his love and caring for these children who had nothing and supplying some of their needs, he would illustrate to them that through love there is hope, even when your life has been totally devastated. He also added that the radiance and the smiles he saw in the faces of the children was all the reward he needed this side of eternity.

Over lunch one of the doctors told us of something remarkable that happens quite frequently, and the staff were still unable to fathom how it works – a blind girl and a deaf girl become friends and develop some kind of communication.

The school had a small shop that sold sweets, toys, and magazines, most of them donated by charities. The two friends would go to the shop together, where the blind girl would gesture to the deaf girl, and the deaf girl would make noises to the blind girl.

The deaf girl would choose two items and the blind girl would pay the shopkeeper. They both came out of the shop with what they wanted and still the school doctors and staff didn't know how they had done it.

As we finished filming in the afternoon, we were taken to a small room where a doctor, who specialised in teaching deaf children, was working with a nine-year-old girl. We watched as the doctor got her to make breathy sounds onto a small piece of paper so she could see the paper move as she made the sound.

He said they had made good headway with both sign language and vocal speech with many of the young children, and the school was particularly pleased with the progress of this girl. We thanked him for all he was doing to help these children and as we turned to leave the little girl smiled towards us and formed some words which we didn't understand, but the doctor looked at us and said, 'Renee has just said, "Thank you for coming to see me,"' – and she smiled again.

I'm a fully-grown man from Yorkshire – we don't cry. So why was I unable to see anyone through the tears?

It had been an uplifting day, the journey back to Harare was very quiet. The memories and laughter of those children still live with me.

Death and Cricket

A man of the cloth can have a remarkable effect on a film crew. Directors who are normally decisive, confident and moderately clear, can become hesitant, awkward and in some cases downright sluggish. The scale of intellectual malaise is usually directly related to the rank or position of the gentlemen being interviewed. I say 'gentlemen' because in my experience 98% have been male.

The scale operates as follows. A Free Church minister would not prove any problem for most television directors, as they believe their university degree in Oriental Languages or heraldry in the fifteenth century will get them through any intellectual confrontation. The average Reverend can bowl the occasional googly but does not pose a threat. When one enters the precincts of bishops, archbishops, cardinals and theological scholars one is playing on a totally different wicket, particularly if the cardinals are Jesuit trained, as David Frost found to his cost when interviewing Cardinal Heenan on the Pope's encyclical on 'the Pill'. These people are theological minefields, with intellects of a magnitude such as a mere media mogul would have difficulty comprehending. The debate would not involve budgets, viewing figures or profit. It would however contain references to belief, faith, purpose, a world view, realism, sincerity and truth. The last category would fill the mogul's with fear, and uncertainty. Sincerity and truth are alien to their work ethic and ought not to be entertained.

The trouble always seems to lie at the feet of the TV network or production company who set up the confrontation in the first place. Often, only a researcher, or keen production assistant will have spoken to the prelate, and found them to be charming and in many cases very good company. There is, in most cases, a good reason for this observation – they *are* charming, and in most cases very good company. The researcher returns to base with the truth, and in a few weeks the film crew will enter the theological portals of the said prelate to record the interview.

Death and Cricket

Film crews are not known or paid for their intellectual prowess; after all, we are craftsmen and women whose skills lie in setting up tripods, focusing a lens, carrying heavy metal boxes and turning on a recorder. Conversation tends to revolve around football, designer trainers, designer labels, the latest film equipment and 'have you seen my new motor' followed by, 'you will not believe how much I drank at...' and so on. Food can often occupy a lot of discussion time. These innocents could be easy pickings for the likes of an archbishop, but not so; these gentlemen of the cloth turn out to be – charming, courteous, and in many cases very friendly people.

At this point any reader with a fear of eternity should either put the book down or move on to the next chapter.

It was such an occasion, which brought a crew and myself to visit a bishop in the West Country. We entered the grounds of the Bishop, a man in his mid-fifties with a passion for cricket and a keen supporter of Tottenham Hotspur and Somerset County cricket team.

The director was an eager young chap, who thought that as it was a warm day and the forecast was for fine weather with a very light breeze it would be a jolly good idea to film the interview outside. The director, to my surprise, asked me if the wind and the distant traffic noise would interfere with the sound. I assured him he wouldn't hear any and thanked him for his consideration (a quality seldom observed in young male directors).

As I shared the Bishop's passion for cricket it gave us an obvious topic of conversation when I was fitting him with a radio microphone. Our memories of the game ran almost parallel as we were of a similar age, and very soon we were into Test matches at Lord's, Fred Trueman, Don Bradman and deep fine leg. We had just got through a couple of maiden overs from Dennis Lillee when the director asked the Bishop if he would like to go over the line and length of the questions he would be asking him. The Bishop thanked him, and said that it would not be necessary as he preferred things off the cuff, but if he would like to toss him a 'googly' or a 'Chinaman' at any point, it would keep him on his toes.

The interview got under way with questions about childhood

and teenage years, which were designed to relax the Bishop. Questions followed about girlfriends, miniskirts and quite naturally, cricket. He did tell the story related by Dickie Bird, of Fred Trueman, where if Yorkshire were taking the field at the beginning of a match, the entire team plus two umpires would be out at the wicket, all except Trueman. I should point out that at the particular time Dickie Bird was remembering, Trueman was quite possibly the fastest and certainly the most ferocious pace bowler in the world. Trueman could always be found at the boundary fence by the gate the two opening batsmen would be walking through. As the batsmen came through the gate Trueman could be heard to say, quite loudly, 'I wouldn't bother closing t'gate, tha'll not be staying out there long.' The Bishop had many good stories to tell, and the crew were happy for him to continue, but the director steered the questions back to the Church.

The next question assumed that the Bishop had gone to university, read Classics, and then immediately gone into the church as a chosen career move.

'I wasn't a Christian when I was at university, I was more of an agnostic with leanings towards the left and the miners' cause,' said the Bishop.

This was the first googly the director was to receive, his research had missed out on all three points.

'Did you always have leanings towards the left?' asked the director, now missing the obvious question about the Bishop's agnosticism.

'I have always had leanings to the left and since becoming a bishop my leanings have only been encouraged.'

Our director waded through the political mire he found himself in and finally attempted to escape with some degree of questioning logic by asking, 'Does the Church find it embarrassing that many political leaders discover it necessary to declare their allegiance to God and the Church as soon as they are in a position of power?'

'The leaders who particularly stand out in my memory would be Martin Luther and Oliver Cromwell, both men Christians long before they changed the face of the Western world; they had no need to claim allegiance to the Church or to God as they were already known as men of faith.'

'But they died many years ago, and for most people have very little relevance today,' said our man.

'The translation of the Bible, from Latin into the everyday German of the common people, gave all of them access, for the first time, to a knowledge of God's individual love for each one of them, whether male or female.' The Bishop paused, and our man was in with his next thrust.

'But as a man of the Church you cannot condone Cromwell's sacking of the church buildings?'

The Bishop leant forward slightly, causing a shift in focus, and an intake of breath from the cameraman, sufficient to irritate the director as he felt he had the Bishop on the ropes with his last straight left jab.

'The buildings were no more than carved stones, mortar of sorts, and a number of relics; such materials have little or nothing to do with the Church. Once the Bible was translated from Latin in both Europe and England, into the common language of the people, the New Testament soon revealed to the people what had been hidden from them for centuries. The Church was not the cathedral, monastery, or any building, whether it had a spire or a tower. The Church was and is the people; the very people who had been told for hundreds of years they only had access to God by attending the designated buildings called 'church' whatever the form. These people were now free to worship and to speak to God directly. They could speak individually, or in small groups, or even in large groups; they were still the church God had planned from the beginning. This was a freedom some of the people in England had, but Cromwell was determined to give them political freedom over their everyday lives. The only way Cromwell could bring this political freedom to the people was by removing the King as head of parliament, and although the final result was the removal of the King by execution, this was not as Cromwell wished it to happen.

'After many months of political debate and reason, the King refused to hand control over to the people through elections. Cromwell continued to try and reason with his own people that to remove the King by execution was against the law of God, but finally, and reluctantly, he placed his name on the death certificate. Since that time we have had elections every five years as given to us by Oliver Cromwell, you have the freedom of choice to vote for who you wish without fear of persecution thanks to one man and his followers. His statue, quite rightly, stands outside the Houses of Parliament... now, do we think that covers what it was you were asking me about politicians and allegiance to the Church?' The Bishop then smiled gently; the director didn't, he needed some form of lifebelt.

'I think we should break for lunch,' said the director.

We broke for lunch.

It was obvious from the number of books in the library that this was a well-read man. Three and a half walls, the remaining half had a window overlooking the garden, contained books from floor to ceiling. As I disconnected the radio microphone I asked the Bishop how many books he had, and he thought it was probably just under four thousand on history and theology; the rest of his reading, on cricket and football, was in a reading room upstairs, but this was quite modest by comparison, probably only a couple of hundred books. I asked him if he had read all of his books, 'I imagine I have,' he replied with that gentle smile, and asked me if I ought to be having some lunch.

I joined the others in the kitchen and tackled a smoked salmon and cucumber sandwich in brown bread with the crust cut off – you see, I can go on about food when given the chance.

The cameraman was muttering to the director about the Bishop continually leaning forward and shifting the field of focus, the director was muttering back to the cameraman, asking him not to breathe so loudly when the Bishop did lean forward.

'Couldn't you ask him not to lean forward?' Now the director sighed, and told the cameraman, quite firmly, that the Bishop had already had him on toast in the morning and he did not want to be served up as the main course later on.

'I thought you were getting what you wanted?' mumbled the cameraman.

'I'm sure you did,' said the director quietly, with a degree of irritation.

Two ladies from the parish, who had not only prepared the tasty lunch, but served us in a most welcoming manner, left us

Death and Cricket

and said they would be back with more refreshments around four o'clock.

A few weeks prior to the filming, a certain bishop in the north had thrown doubt on Mary's Virgin Birth of Jesus and his physical Resurrection. Our Bishop in the West Country held a quite opposing belief from the doubting prelate; this was his own particular problem, and it held no sway in Canterbury. Nevertheless, the media quite naturally did not share the same view as the Church, for them this was grist for the mill, and at least a good headline on the front page of a broadsheet, a token heading on page 5 of a tabloid, with the TV news running it in sixth or seventh place following 'Prime Minister has tea at Chequers with pop-star' and 'Tower Bridge raised twice in one day'.

This was all very well, but our man had already been through an attack by a theological missile, and he wished, so very much, not to have a similar experience that afternoon. In most film crews there are always a random number of atheists, but on that day the entire crew was present and showing a lot more interest than would be expected. Perhaps the thought of 'roast director and two veg' had some appeal.

Back in the garden, the weather had held, as promised by Michael Fish; the wind was light, and all was well with the sound department. The director looked at ease, though one could sense a raging turmoil inside, only the cameraman was sighing loudly. The director appeared not to notice and fired the first question at the Bishop.

'As atheism is becoming more apparent these days, particularly with the academics of the world, isn't Christianity nothing more than an emotional crutch for the common people?'

'There have always been atheists and agnostics from the very beginning,' replied the Bishop, 'and not only with the academics. The common man, as you call him, also took pleasure in worshipping images of his own making. Right back in the Old Testament, the Jewish history is littered with brazen images and idols; today the images are still in evidence, they have just changed their shape. Possessions, money, ambition, avarice, television, work and many others have all become idols of self-centredness, which in itself is the very core of atheism.

Death and Cricket

'As for the academics you refer to, I find it difficult to believe that the likes of Galileo, or Dostoyevsky, or possibly the greatest mathematical mind the world has yet known, Blaise Pascal, had a need for Christianity as an emotional crutch. These men were passionate believers in the death and Resurrection of Christ, despite their great intellects.'

The Bishop paused for a moment, our director nodded as if to indicate some degree of understanding, and did look as though he was about to offer a further thought, when the Bishop reminded him not to forget the 'father of science' – Isaac Newton, whose mind and life not only encompassed Christianity, but introduced the world to mathematical and scientific theory of gravitational immensity. Despite the magnitude of thought and genius possessed by these men, all of them knew the inner need of the human race for, as Martin Luther said, 'justification by faith' – and not the fragility of self-justification.

The director motioned with his left hand into space, and then said, 'Whether the Virgin Birth is true or not, Jesus was obviously an astute political figure and great moral teacher, don't you think?'

'You know, from your research, that I believe firmly in the Virgin Birth of Jesus, but as to him being a moral teacher, I think not.'

Now that was it, the director knew he had him over the ropes. He never expected it to be so easy, he knew all he had to do was to hit the Bishop with a few quotes from The Sermon on the Mount and it would be game, set and match. He raised his finger to the sky, and then at the Bishop's chest, in a friendly gesture. The Bishop leant forward again, the cameraman took an intake of breath, and the Bishop continued.

'If he were to be a moral teacher, he would have failed in the purpose for his being on earth. You see, we must look at what he said about himself to determine whom, and what his purpose was. If it is true that he was, as he said, the Son of God who was here to save people for all eternity – it was and is of infinite importance. On the other hand, if it is not true, it was and is of no importance whatsoever, and he can be dismissed as a ranting magician of no value. The one thing Jesus can never be, is

Death and Cricket

moderately important. It is at a point such as this that one has to make a choice, one must recognise the free will we have been given to make any choice, and this one will affect your existence in eternity. You can ignore him as a fool, dismiss him as a demon; or you can believe he is the Son of God and fall at his feet. But don't come forward with any politically correct patronising nonsense about him being a great human teacher. He has not left that open to us. He did not intend to.'

It looked like the 'politically correct patronising' bit was rattling around in the director's head and causing him more than a modicum of unease. After a moment of looking at the cameraman, who just looked back, and playing for time, asked me if the birdsong was too loud; he had noticed one particular shrill moment. I assured him all was absolutely fine. He appeared to be finding some composure, if little of his BBC directorial bearing. To say the expression on his face veered towards 'taut' would be accurate.

'I'm sure you must be aware of the hoax theory, both regarding the Virgin Birth and the Resurrection, which appears to have gathered pace inside the Church at the present time,' he said to the Bishop.

'I am well aware of the doubts which have been put forward in the Church as to the physical Resurrection of Jesus, and also the well-tried hoax theory. We ought to deal with the hoax theory first as it will not take very long. The disciples are probably the best point at which to start, having been with Jesus on many occasions after the Resurrection. He met with two of them on the road to Emmaus, and then with ten of them in a room where they checked the injuries to his hands. Later while they were fishing on Lake Galilee, Jesus called to them from the shore. He then proceeded to cook breakfast for himself and the disciples. On each of the occasions mentioned Jesus ate food with them. A ghost, a spirit, an apparition does not eat food. This was the human Jesus they had known before the crucifixion, this was the Jesus seen by many hundreds during the next few weeks.'

'It must be remembered that these are the same disciples who later gave their lives for their faith, some being prepared to die in fire and crucifixion, and others crucified upside down. If this had been a hoax, one of them, if not most of them would have come clean and said as the fire was being lit; or the nails about to be hammered in, "Hang on, just one minute…" But not one of them did.'

'Charles Colson, one of Nixon's senior aides at the time of Watergate in the 1970s made an interesting remark after the presidency collapsed. Looking back over the events he said, "he found it worth noting that during the intense pressure of the investigation, the finest legal minds in America could not hold the lie for more than three weeks". If the Resurrection had been a hoax, someone would have blown the cover.'

'When I think of the empires throughout history with their might, wealth, military power and philosophy, the span of time they covered was quite minimal. The Babylonians, the Persians, the Greeks, the Romans, and each one with their own gods and deities, at best couldn't muster much more than a hundred years. Christianity has grown from a handful of people, a few fishermen, a tax collector, a doctor and a tent-maker to a membership of over one and a half billion in 2,000 years, with the Cross of Christ and the physical Resurrection at the centre of the faith. The fact that the Christian Church still exists is likely to be the best evidence of its validity, and for us to write letters today which bear a date still linked to that first Easter. Our Bishop from the north could do well to remember he only has a job because Christ was crucified, and that he rose from the dead on that first Easter. When he gets his next pay cheque, the date on that cheque is directly related to that first Easter.'

'I trust that answers your question satisfactorily? If we had a couple of days I could be more precise.'

'Do you believe in Hell, and if so what kind of Hell?'

Some of us looked at each other, and thought, He's finally lost it, does he mean the kind of hell he's been through today, or is this a desperate man who has decided his career is over and caution has been thrown to the wind? The rest of the crew looked eager: perhaps this was going to be 'roast director with two veg' as the main course.

'I take it you are not referring to the frenetic remarks overheard when Spurs have lost again at home for the third time:

Death and Cricket

"It was hell out there – the defence was shot to pieces"? I gather it's more likely that you mean Hell stretching from death through a never-ending eternity.'

The director nodded.

'I only used the glib introduction to draw attention to a gross misuse of language. Today the word hell is used totally out of context, as is Jesus Christ. "She gave him hell" – "It was a hell of a long way" – harmless, descriptive references to the magnitude of anger or of distance. Not so. As with Jesus, our language has become so debased that the *Oxford English Dictionary* defines the meaning, first – an exclamation of surprise, dismay, etc. and second – (name of the founder of the Christian religion). In fact, look back to the early eighteenth century, Voltaire, the French writer and philosopher, stated that within two hundred years the name of Jesus Christ would not be remembered by anyone. Now, after almost three hundred years, the name of Jesus is remembered and used by millions every day, whereas not too many remember Voltaire. It's also interesting, don't you think, that Confucius, Buddha or Krishna are not used as any form of exclamation – why pick Jesus?

'The only possible reason I can come up with is that Jesus is the only one linking death with the endless state of eternity, and a final judgement. It is also noticeable that those who have used their freedom of will and made a choice, believing that Jesus is who he said he is – the Son of God – these people do not use "Jesus" as a form of exclamation. Only those whose choice has placed self-will, self-interest, and self-justification appear to use both "Jesus" and "Hell" as forms of description or dismay. This is in no way condemning those who have made the alternative choice, it is simply pointing out that one group of people have a sense and understanding of eternity, whereas the other group do not. In many cases they find they have no interest in death or eternity – it is just the end.'

'Many friends of mine who are atheists fall into this last category and have no concept of Heaven, Hell or eternity, and some remind me yet again that "there is no God". They are never too keen to hear that God does not believe in atheists. We are told in Ecclesiastes, Chapter three, that God has placed eternity in the

Death and Cricket

hearts of all people, and this is something my atheist friends quietly wrestle with a lot of the time: What if…? Could it be true that Jesus…?

'Forgive me for posing a question for you,' continued the Bishop, 'but I am occasionally asked, How can a God, who loves us unconditionally, send us to Hell?

'My reply is always, God did not create Hell for us, God does not send us to Hell, we save Him the trouble, we choose to go there. Hell was only created for Satan and his demonic angels at the end of time where they will writhe in an eternal agony, as recorded in Revelation. It is we, God's creation, who make that choice, and go there to spend eternity in agony with Satan. God has given us free will to choose our own relationships, with whoever on earth, and whoever in eternity. His love is such that he aches for us to be with Him forever. So much so, He placed His own Son on a cross to die in our place, and is grieved beyond measure when we choose the eternal alternative.' He paused then added, 'I apologise for injecting a question which you obviously had prepared.'

'Not at all,' said the director, 'Please, do go on.'

'Hell, I believe, does not come in the shape or form introduced to us in Renaissance art, or in graphic novels. I'm afraid it is far worse, more terrifying, and light years beyond our most hideous imaginings. At the point of death all atheists will discover they were wrong. They will be in the presence of Almighty God and His Son, Jesus. A video of their lives will be shown for all to see, and then they will be asked the reasons for the choices they made. Self-justification suddenly appears to have no value or purpose. They will realise that the Glory and Wonder of Heaven, they now have a glimpse of, is all they will ever have, as they are taken to spend eternity in the place of their choosing – Hell. They may be expecting "the lake of fire and brimstone" but that would be mild torment. They find themselves sealed in a void that seems like a bland room with no windows, and no doors, and no light. They are surrounded by nowhere, travelling to nowhere. They are left with the one thing they enjoyed most on earth – themselves. This is solitary confinement, forever, and ever, and ever; this does not end, in fact it is a state of timeless eternity. A state in which they had shown no interest, but chosen to inhabit. To have nobody with whom to justify their actions or thoughts, removes a previous part of their life – but this was not life – this was and is eternity, this was endless. They find the space around never changes in its blandness; there is nobody else, there is nothing except for the horror and intense pain in the knowledge that God does exist, of having glimpsed the Wonder and Glory surrounding Him, and the Knowledge and Glory they will never be part of – ever. The knowledge that they had been wrong, the knowing that self-justification meant for nothing, the knowing that there are no atheists in *Hell*, the knowledge their voice has no purpose, the knowledge that all they have is of no purpose, and when their reason has examined every detail of their existence and being for ten thousand years, and found the answer is always – nothing. The *scream* begins… and continues… and continues… forever and forever… and forever… and forever… there is nobody to hear… nobody to listen… there is nobody… that is your choice.'

After a pause, the Bishop remarked 'That's how it could be, from my understanding.'

'But then we have the wonderful offer God made to us on the cross, of his Son crucified in our place, paying the price for all evil ever thought or committed. You know, when Jesus died on the cross it wasn't the crucifixion that killed him, it was losing sight of his Father's face for the only time in his life. His Father turned away and poured the sin of the world for all time on to his own Son. Jesus died, not through crucifixion, but because his heart exploded with the weight of our sin, your sin, and my sin. It used to take anything up to three days for someone to die on the cross, but if required, death could be hastened by breaking the legs of the victims. It was such an occasion on that day, as the Jewish festival would begin the following day, the legs of the two men crucified with Jesus were broken, but when they came to Jesus they found that he had already died, so they pierced his side with a spear just as a precaution and blood and water poured from him. Jesus had been dead long enough for the clot and serum to separate. This is a price beyond my deepest imaginings, that this was done for me and for you, God's unconditional love giving us

Death and Cricket

the basis of our faith, our stepping-stone into eternity and life everlasting with Him. This is Total Forgiveness offered to us, you and me, by God through the death of His Son on a cross at Calvary. It's hardly surprising that John Newton finished his hymn 'Amazing Grace' with:

> When we've been there ten thousand years
> Bright shining as the sun
> There's no less time to sing God's praise
> Than when we first begun.'

The Bishop looked at the director and said, 'I doubt there's anything more I can add after that.'

The director was silent for a while before thanking him for his time and hospitality.

The cameraman told the director that the Bishop had moved forward a few times making focus a problem.

The director looked at the cameraman and said, 'I've just been taken through the bowels of Hell and lifted into the Glory of Heaven, don't talk to me about focus!'

The two ladies from the parish arrived with tea and simnel cake.

On the journey back to London the director was particularly quiet, the cameraman was from the West Country, so fortunately was in his own transport and couldn't fascinate us with the nuances of focus. The main topic, however, was not football or designer labels, but how does a bloke like the Bishop have time to read all those books, know so much about sport, make religion interesting, and do his normal job.

'I did find him a bit frightening on Hell,' said a voice.

Then it was quiet.

'Collar the Lot' (Winston Churchill)

Lavinia Warner, a director with an interest and substantial knowledge of World War II, asked Martin and myself to work on a film involving the Jews and Italians living in the UK prior to 1939.

It was 1982, and many of the contributors were still only middle-aged.

When war broke out, and Winston Churchill was put in charge, the War Cabinet decided to collect all aliens who had lived in Britain for the last ten years and to ship them to prison camps in Australia, Canada and The Isle of Man. Churchill, having second thoughts, felt ten years wasn't sufficient, and issued his famous order to 'Collar the Lot'.

In thirty-eight years of working in television documentary, I have never found anyone or any company remotely equal to Lavinia Warner in her detailed research. On a film such as this, which carries emotions, memories and modern history at the forefront, precise and accurate research is essential and invaluable.

David was then living and working in Australia with his wife Gill, who was working closely alongside Mel Gibson on *Mad Max Beyond the Thunderdome*. She mentioned later 'this was a good time in her life'. Martin was working with a variety of assistants, and Dave Knill was up for this one.

The schedule was for the film to be interview-led, and in as many of the original locations as possible from among those that hadn't been bulldozed.

Our first group were three Italians, two who were born in the UK and one who came with his family in the mid-1920s. We were in a restaurant in Soho, which was then owned by one of them. They were pleasant, relaxed and had quite gripping stories to tell us.

The two younger men remembered being woken in the night by a banging on the door of the house they were living in. Their parents came and told them to get dressed as they had to leave the house. What they didn't say was that they had to leave the country.

In two days, they were on a ship heading for Canada. The teenagers knew there was a war on but were puzzled why shipping them from Liverpool to Canada would help the war effort. They were also intrigued to discover that the majority of the other passengers were also Italians with a few Jews for company.

The British soldiers travelling with them started to organise them into groups of about thirty. When the groups had been sorted out, the soldiers would take one group at a time and get them to bring their cases and bags on to the deck, where the soldiers would search them for anything incriminating or 'useful'.

The soldiers put anything they felt was of no value or purpose back in the cases, and threw them overboard. The Italians complained, quite naturally, not at the loss of their baggage, but at the trail being left for any German U boat to follow – it would lead them right to their ship. The soldiers apparently paid no attention, after all these were only Eyeties – what could they know?

In less than two hours the ship had been torpedoed and hundreds were drowned.

The men told us that the fortunate ones who were saved were taken back to Liverpool, where they were held for a few days.

In less than a week they were all on another ship for Canada again.

Two days into the voyage another batch of soldiers sorted them into groups, checked through their bags and cases for items of destruction they might have picked up in the holding camp outside Liverpool, and then threw the bags and cases overboard.

The Italians pleaded with them not to continue, and again explained why, but to no avail. Within an hour, the torpedoes struck and hundreds more died.

Back in Liverpool, the survivors were put on another ship, this time heading for Australia, which mercifully arrived safely, seven weeks later.

We shared some wine and delicious pasta with the three gentlemen, thanked them for telling us about their experiences during the war, and for their remarkable understanding and forgiving nature.

★

The Amadeus String Quartet

The Quartet were rehearsing at a house in north London, and Lavinia thought this would be a good venue to film the interview and to record them playing.

For me, this was about as close as one gets to pure joy whilst working.

All four were Jews, and had been interned in the prison camp on the Isle of Man.

Like many remarkable coincidences in life, it took place in the most unusual circumstances. One of the musicians, I believe it was Peter, was sitting by his hut in the camp, and playing his violin. He told us that he hadn't decided to play the Mendelssohn violin concerto, but just happened to be. Obviously he was only playing the violin part, as there was no orchestra around. When he got to a section where the orchestra would have come in he stopped playing and hummed the orchestral part in his head. He was doing this when he heard another violin playing the orchestral section a short distance away. When the orchestral part had finished he continued the violin part, only to discover the accompaniment from the 'orchestral violin' filling in all the correct sections.

The two men greeted each other and fifty per cent of a quartet was formed. During the period of the war, two other men, one who happened to play viola and the other cello, both at virtuoso level, joined the two violins. One of the greatest string quartets the world has known was formed in a prison camp on the Isle of Man.

What wasn't realised until well after the war, was that the prison camp for aliens on the Isle of Man could possibly have been the best Open University yet to be found.

In the early 1930s many university professors and intellectuals, along with professional musicians and writers, had left Germany and Austria, as they were aware of what National Socialism could become. Jews in particular were leaving for Britain and the USA. Consequently when Churchill gave the order to 'collar the lot' the Isle of Man became the enforced home for many professors, university lecturers, teachers, writers, economists and industrialists. It didn't take long for a collection of thinkers of this excellence to organise workshops and study groups, which not only passed the time, but also helped to stabilise emotions, and provide a purpose. It was these groups that educated and produced the likes of economist and statistician Sir Klaus Moser, along with Tiny Rowland and many others who now work and assist in the running of the City of London. As one of them said with a wry smile, 'I have heard some people say, I suppose we ought to thank Hitler – I think not.'

Lavinia did find one retired journalist in his nineties, who in 1914 had worked for the *Manchester Guardian*.

He told us, 'As a Jew and a journalist in 1914, I was not surprised to be taken to the prison camp on the Isle of Man at the outbreak of the First World War.'

However, what did surprise him was to be picked up again in 1940, and shipped back to the Isle of Man camp for a second term, in World War II.

I suppose the highlight of the film for me was to sail from Liverpool to the Isle of Man. This was to interview some of the residents who remembered living on the island during the war, and also to take a couple of ex-prisoners with us to share in their memories of the camp.

The reason it was so special for me, was the memory of my dad taking us to the Isle of Man from Liverpool on the *King Orry* or the *Viking* when we were kids.

I remember the absolute thrill in 1982 standing on the quay of the Princess landing stage and seeing the *King Orry*, still sailing, and berthing in sight of the Royal Liver Building, the giant birds on the two towers still as much of a mystery to me as when I was a kid.

The only slight regret I felt was being unable to send a card from the Isle of Man to the 'bottle blonde at the Locarno Ballroom' simply to let her know *I had made it!*

Situations Best Avoided

There are many times when a basic hunch ought to tell you 'this is not a good idea', and perhaps after thirty-five years of working in such a 'sincere' industry, one could assume I would have learnt many lessons. Not so.

In the spring of 1994, a much loved director Susanna White asked me to be part of a project for which she thought I would be eminently suitable.

The subject of the documentary was a competition run by a photographic magazine where male readers could enter photos of their wives or girlfriends nude or semi-naked. Both were to be filmed and interviewed in action to explain their reasons for taking part.

The crew had visited quite a few couples and gathered some interesting footage for the programme when we were asked to visit a home in Essex, where a lady was very keen for us to include her in the film. This lady didn't have a husband or a boyfriend, but her local chemist had taken some appropriate snaps of her in various outfits, or not, as the fancy took her.

When we arrived at her home in Gants Hill, the lady – Sandra, who looked a very compact 45-year-old but in a good light could have got away with 35 – showed us into the front room. She was chatty and pleasant, if a little excitable, and immediately showed us the pictures taken by her friend the chemist. A cursory glance made it obvious at the outset that abandon had been to the fore and discretion completely underplayed. Sandra appeared to be most pleased with the chemist's work and recommended we should interview him; our director made a polite reply.

After interviewing Sandra we made arrangements to see her the following week to film her in some of the costumes, or not, and then go to a dance at her favourite club even deeper into Essex than we had yet been. As we were preparing to leave a large male, with muscles, let himself in with his own keys and was introduced to us as Sandra's 'boyfriend' – of three days. He was of

Situations Best Avoided

continental extraction, a builder, 6 foot 3½ inches tall, and built like a brick outside loo. I guess he weighed in at 16 to 17 stone with not an ounce of fat on him, and had hands as big as buckets. As the crew drove back to base we all agreed he was around the late forties, was well able to look after himself, and was not best pleased to see us with his new 'girlfriend'.

The following week we turned up again at Sandra's house only to find a totally distraught lady whose 'continental, 6 foot 3½ inch boyfriend, with muscles had left her that morning, with no intention of coming back if she was to continue with the filming. Maybe it was her fifteen minutes of fame, so she had decided to continue with the filming. She thought she had a beautiful body for a 45-year-old and felt others should have the pleasure of sharing it with her; unfortunately this view was not shared by the 'continental, 6 foot 3½ inch boyfriend'.

Sandra then had a 'good idea'. Perhaps if she got dressed up for the dance at her favourite club in deepest Essex and we didn't do the filming of her in some of her costumes, then her boyfriend wouldn't mind and he would return. Susanna, our director, thought this was a 'spiffing idea' and put the kettle on whilst Sandra prepared for her night out in Essex.

An hour later Sandra came downstairs ready for her few minutes of fame at an Essex nightclub. I have to add that we all left with a sense of relief that there was still no sign of the boyfriend.

The atmosphere at the club was good and the management seemed pleased to have us there. Sandra was dancing with people she knew and we did a bit of filming followed by a short interview with her. At midnight Susanna called it a day, which pleased Sandra as she was still a bit anxious about the boyfriend and just wanted to get back home. We wrapped the gear in about twenty minutes and loaded into our individual cars. Sandra, in the meantime, had been talking with Susanna about getting home, and I was asked if I could give her a lift as it was on my way and only a couple of hundred yards off the A12. During the time I was being asked this, Chris the cameraman, was standing behind Susanna and Sandra shaking his head, and mouthing to me, *don't do it, don't do it!*

Situations Best Avoided

At this point, thirty-five years of experience ought to have kicked in and told me, Chris is right, say 'No'. So I looked them both in the eyes and said, 'Okay its only just off the A12, it won't take long.' Well, my mum and dad said I should always help a maiden if in distress.

As I got into my car with Sandra I could see Chris driving off in his Volvo, still shaking his head. On the drive back, Sandra kept telling me how grateful she was and did I think she looked good when she was dancing and did she look good on the camera and was the interview all right and did I think she looked thirty, because... had I noticed she had a very young body?

As we approached her house she let out a muffled scream and gabbled, 'He's back – there's his van!' I said, 'Well, that's good, you must be pleased.' Sandra got out of the car and said, 'You've got to come and tell him how good I was.'

I thought, Hang about, that's the last thing I'm going to tell him. As far as he was concerned I'd been drooling over his girlfriend's naked or almost naked body with the rest of the crew, and now I'd come back to take full advantage of the situation.

'Come on – come on, you've got to tell him!' Her voice was getting louder and one or two bedroom lights were going on in the neighbours' houses; after all, it was 1 o'clock in the morning.

I got out of the car and Sandra hurried ahead of me to open the door. She went in and called out a name, I couldn't tell what the name was, but with that well-known family tradition for cowardice coming to the fore, coupled with a fighting weight of 12½ stone of mainly soft white flab, I felt this was not a particularly good time to ask. Sandra then came back to the open door and beckoned me in. 'Come in – come on and tell him how good I was.'

Like a fool, I went in and there was this giant sitting in a white beach robe. As he stood up he appeared to get larger and said, 'I've just showered, I'm ready for bed.'

Now in all honesty, I don't think his comments were addressed to me, but I did say, "ood!' (The 'g' seemed to disappear down my throat.) Sandra still insisted that I tell him how good she was, I backed towards the door, which fortunately was still open.

'She really was m-mmod,' I said in a hurried tone. I hesitated, and thought, Did I just say *m-mmod*, did I really say *m-mmod*?

The 'continental, 17-stone giant at 6 foot 3½ inches, with muscles' appeared to move towards me and said 'Goodnight.' I noticed the 'G' hadn't disappeared down his throat, and I moved smartly through the door and disappeared into the night. It was only as I walked to the car I realised how much I was shaking. We Desmonds have never responded well in the face of terror.

Chris Morphet, how right you were!

Boredom and Vultures

Boredom arrives in unlikely shapeless forms, is no respecter of persons, and often comes when least expected. It turns up at locations as a tedious malaise, with little to recommend it. Philip Larkin, the poet, summed it up accurately – 'Nothing, like something, happens anywhere.'

The Volvo Estate purchased by Chris Morphet 'the cameraman' had the fresh leather smell of a new car, and all the Swedish luxury that could be offered without being vulgar. Chris, Carlo and Keith were off to a hospital in Stoke on Trent, where Jeremy and Emma – the director and producer – had been for a few days setting up the filming. This particular hospital was, at that time, one of the few in the country that always had a consultant in the A&E department 24 hours a day. This accounted for speed and accuracy of diagnosis, plus the correct treatment. They wanted some of this high-speed medical stuff on camera and Channel 4 thought it would make a cracking – 'fly on the wall' documentary, don't you know. Not a hint of boredom in that.

Chris 'the cameraman', Carlo and Keith had worked on many hospital-based programmes before and knew what to expect. Trauma, trauma – plenty of trauma – no worries. Blood – sometimes lots of blood, the crew could handle blood – no problem. The surgeon's knife in glands, rapid response, instant pressure, medical staff in top gear, and nurses – there's always the nurses. Nurses in clean blue or white uniforms, rustling about, and being simply wonderful. At his age, you'd think Keith could hold himself in check in the presence of white rustling uniforms. Alas, not so; how sad.

The crew met Jeremy and Emma at the hospital, and were immediately told they should have been there two days ago. Last week would have been even better. Chests and stomachs were opened at the drop of a scalpel, bits and pieces removed, polished and put back. Corpses queued up at the morgue, limbs

Boredom and Vultures

amputated, a doctor got attacked by a patient – and that was just Monday. This tends to be the pattern when chasing trauma for TV – it's always happened before the crew got there.

They set up their stall in the quietest corner of A&E, not that there is a quiet corner in A&E, but they tried to be out of the way. Two ladies in white, who rustled a bit and smiled, provided a few chairs. They were shooting on film, not video, so Keith had the luxury of not being attached to Chris 'the cameraman' by an umbilical cable, and had the freedom to wander wherever he wished, to record whatever 'trauma' was passing by.

Now as it happened, their location in A&E was quite crucial, although they didn't realise this at the time, until one of the nurses told them that the telephone on the wall opposite was the 'red alert' phone for any incoming emergencies. They liked this, as they were only about 15 feet from the phone and could see it and hear it, if it rang. On the wall above the telephone was a large 24-hour clock, which was to become a major feature in the lives of the crew over the next eight days.

Not a lot happened during the next couple of days, which gave the crew time to become acquainted with the medical staff and meet the consultants. The 'red alert' phone had rung three times, but none of the calls rated as red alert. Fortunately, Chris, Carlo, Keith and Jeremy do not tell jokes, Emma had been known to, but the crew always tried to rein her in whenever possible.

When they hadn't seen each other for two or three weeks, there were things to discuss – manly things, questions to be asked: Where are Spurs in the league? Is Alan Sugar for the chop? Vital information to exchange… The chairs provided by the ladies who rustled a bit and smiled, gave them an ideal spot to catch up on all the news.

Days three and four still did not produce much activity, although there was a new staff nurse on duty who ran A&E with military precision, and had eyes which penetrated like lasers. She was terrific. The crew just hoped when 'trauma' did arrive, it would be on her shift.

Waiting for the unknown can become tedious, especially when the catch-up news has been repeated a few times and food in the

Boredom and Vultures

hospital canteen becomes a major highlight of the day.

It's usually about this time that one of the crew cracks, and feels a desperate need to tell some totally unrelated account of people, who, totally unknown to anyone, were about to embark on some trivial activity. This time, apparently some neighbours, who hadn't long been in the area, had just finished building a swimming pool in their back garden.

The 24-hour clock read 15:07.

The new neighbours were certainly new, and people with polished horizons. They were most keen that the neighbourhood had a jolly good look at their swimming pool, but unfortunately the pool required some cleaning after the workmen had finished building the pool.

Did any of us know a safe cleaning solution for outdoor swimming pools?

The clock read 15:09.

Various cleaning fluids had been mentioned, when mercifully, the 'red alert' phone rang. Like finely coiled springs, the crew, with SAS precision, sprang into action and leapt towards the medic answering the phone. No trauma, only a motorcyclist with a broken leg. Chris 'the cameraman' was by now getting desperate, and pleaded with Jeremy to let him film it, if only to get something in the can. Keith was thinking, Please let's film it, if only to escape the trauma at the swimming pool. Jeremy was adamant, this wasn't trauma, well it might be for the guy on the motorbike, but not for Channel 4.

It was now 15:18.

The crew went back to the chairs with the adrenalin still pumping from a near miss, and sat down, desperately hoping no one would remember the man and his swimming pool, or his cleaning fluids. After an hour and a half of watching the A&E staff rustle and crackle about their work area, doing the impossible for the NHS, Jeremy suddenly came through the door doing a brilliant impression of a vulture. Jeremy said that the crew looked 'much like vultures, who hadn't eaten for a week, sitting on a branch waiting for prey'. It should be pointed out, that Jeremy was born and grew up in Kenya, so he knows, better than any, what a vulture looks like coming into land and settling. The crew simply fell around laughing, along with the nursing staff.

The 24-hour clock said 16:51: time for a cup of tea in the canteen.

Hopes soared when they arrived back at A&E. An old lady of 94 had fallen down her stone cellar steps and was severely bruised, with a few deep cuts. She had been found by her daughter, who had called the ambulance, the paramedics were bringing her in, as they spoke, and transferred her to one of the theatre tables. The lady did, indeed, look as though she had taken on Mike Tyson – and lost. The bruising and swelling around the eyes was alarming, and the cut on her cheek pretty bad, but despite this she was quite chatty.

The staff nurse was taking the details from the lady's daughter, and the doctor was inspecting the damage. 'Were you going down the cellar to get a bottle of Beaujolais?' he asked. The lady looked at him and said, 'No, I'd already drunk it – that's why I fell down the cellar steps.'

The crew hung around until about 9 o'clock, when thankfully Jeremy called it a 'wrap' for the day, as Keith had just started to tell them, and in detail only known to a Yorkshireman, that he had put up a new clothes line in the back yard, a couple of days earlier, and you probably don't know this, but when you tie a bowline, it's essential you must always... Chris smiled sympathetically, and his eyes glazed over... Jeremy said 'Goodnight' to the nurses, and the crew headed back to their hotel.

*

When day seven and eight turned up and they still didn't have 'trauma' it was decided if nothing happened that day, to return to London, 'assess our strategy' – whatever that entailed – and plan a return visit at some time.

It was now day eight and 10:02 on the A&E clock.

The phone was still silent, but looked a bit like this:

(rough sketch to pass some time)

By now, even the fly on the wall had lost interest.
'Did you get wet this morning, when we arrived?'
'Yes, I was with you.'
'I got soaked through – they didn't say it was going to rain.'
'It hardly matters what they said, it did rain, and we both got wet.'
'I got really drenched.'
'I know you did, I was with you.'
Emma came in. 'Did you two get wet this morning when you got here?'
'Yes.'
'Both of you – were you together?'
'Yes.'
'But I didn't get as wet as him, he got really drenched.'
What were they doing? These were grown-up people, talking inanely about the weather. It hardly mattered how wet anyone was, except some time had passed, and still nothing had happened.
The clock read 10:06.
Chris 'the cameraman' turned up with a copy of the *Daily Mirror*, and reminded the crew again that he only buys the *Mirror* for the sports coverage. Chris may not know it, but they had noticed him reading other pages as well... but hadn't told him.
Chris thought Spurs could hold their own against Manchester United at White Hart Lane that coming Saturday.

Boredom and Vultures

A doctor walked through A&E who hadn't been seen before, and who looked a lot like James Cagney, which prompted Keith to relate, yet again, about the time he had worked with James Cagney on the film *Ragtime*. Attempts were made to slow him down, or stop him, but once a Bradford lad gets into full flow about the great and the good who've passed him by, well, it's all over and done with.

Carlo gave Keith one of his looks, and said 'Luther K, please, do us a favour.' Carlo often called Keith 'Luther K' as a term of affection; after all it was his first name. Sometimes, however, Carlo would use it in a cautionary manner, and this was one of those occasions.

A student nurse in subdued blue tried to offer encouragement, by telling Emma that a youth with a dodgy ingrowing toenail was about to arrive in A&E. Emma looked at Jeremy and shook her head, Jeremy looked at Chris, and shook his head. Chris informed Carlo and Keith about the toenail, and shook his head. Carlo looked at Keith and, shaking his head, said, 'A toenail – I think not.'

Carlo was going to get his friend to service his BMW, which he bought in Rome. Carlo is from Rome, you know.

Jeremy arrived back doing another stunning impression of a vulture coming into land. It was the head and neck movement that made it so real, and then the beady eye scouring the horizon of A&E for nourishment, or even a little trauma.

The clock on the wall, read 10:44.

The clock looked a bit like this – if anyone's interested:

(another rough sketch to pass more time)

143

Boredom and Vultures

'Did you have the kippers at breakfast?'
'No.'
'Are you sure you didn't have the kippers?'
'Yes.'
'I thought you had the kippers... If you didn't have the kippers, what did you have?'
'Poached egg on toast.'
'Poached egg on toast looks nothing like kippers.'
'I know, and they taste more like poached egg.'
'I thought you had kippers.'
10:56.

A nurse came and told the crew that an Indian woman had just been brought into A&E suffering from hyperventilation. That was all Chris needed to hear. He grabbed the camera and hurried through to the treatment area. Once Chris smells 'blood' he's his own man; the camera was almost on his shoulder when he leapt into the air like a hurdler. Chris had spotted a lady in a brightly coloured sari lying on a bed, with some medical staff around her. The lady had a brown paper bag on her head, completely covering her face. Due to the bag, the lady had no idea what was going on around her, other than medical staff were caring for her, and talking medical talk. Everything seemed to go into slow motion – Chris was still airborne – the crew were almost at the bed – the consultant had just arrived – and the staff nurse was giving him the details of the case, telling him that the Indian lady's two daughters were in reception waiting for some news of their mother. It was about then that Chris landed on the lady.

The staff simply looked up, saw it was Chris, and continued chatting about medical things. To the A&E staff, nothing peculiar had happened; after all they had known the crew for eight days and had discovered within twenty minutes of the first day that they were a pretty odd bunch. Chris had told them, in some detail, of the exploits at other hospitals the crew had visited. As well as his hours of devout worship at White Hart Lane, his charity cycle rides had been detailed, including the London to Brighton annual cycle run, conquering the 'dreaded' Ditchling Beacon, no less than six times. Fully grown men have been known to die on that hill...

Boredom and Vultures

This was a man, no medical personnel of whatever clout, would dare tangle with.

Chris 'the cameraman' had now straddled the lady, and the crew were all in top gear, filming the consultant going about his business. The lady, meanwhile, must have been wondering, from the inside of her brown paper bag, what part of the treatment entailed having an unseen moving weight pressing down on her anatomy.

Jeremy was talking to the consultant while he worked, who explained that the paper bag over the head was not to prevent the patient seeing what was going on, but to cause them to inhale some of their own carbon dioxide, which would help them breathe more easily.

Now it was slowly dawning on the crew that this under any circumstances couldn't be classed as trauma. At the same moment, Emma noticed two young Indian girls in their late teens, both in vividly coloured saris standing at the bottom of the bed, their mouths open, and staring at the back of a man with a camera on his shoulder, who was on top of their mother, who was wearing a brown paper bag over her head. Like their mother, they must have questioned this particular mode of treatment.

Emma whispered to Jeremy, who whispered to Chris, who looked over his shoulder, grinned and climbed off the bed. Jeremy looked at Carlo and Keith, and with a vulture-like gesture of the head, indicated that it would be a good move if they were to clear off.

The fly on the wall could only be wondering *'What are they doing?'*

Emma made token apologies to the Indian lady and her daughters.

Jeremy consulted the consultant.

That afternoon, the crew drove back to London.

Eleven days later it appeared that 'strategy had been assessed' and Emma phoned the crew to say everything was on again – 'See you in Stoke on Trent in two days.'

Chris's new Volvo still smelt of fresh leather, and after one comfort break, the old hands arrived back at the hospital.

Boredom and Vultures

Once again they were told on arrival that they should have been there last week, as A&E did have great trauma. The way the scene was described, it was obviously the greatest trauma any hospital A&E department could ever experience, and if only the Channel 4 crew had been there – they wouldn't have needed to come back now.

Either the nice rustling ladies in white had placed the chairs for the crew exactly as last time, or the chairs had simply been left out for them, knowing there was no point in moving them as they would be back.

The clock was still there, as was the telephone, which remained silent the more it was looked at.

'17:44' was staring at the crew, and Jeremy decided to pull them out so they could have an early start in the morning.

The staff nurse with the laser eyes was on duty the following morning, so the unit all felt this had to be the day. Trauma must be imminent.

The day passed – no trauma.

The next three days passed, and still no trauma.

Jeremy and Emma began to feel the pressure. After all, it was they who had sold the project to Channel 4, and to all concerned it did seem like a good idea. Jeremy was heard to say on one occasion, that without trauma, the future looked as dim as a Toc H lamp.

Day five arrived and all was quiet. A new intake of student doctors arrived, which proved to be a welcome distraction for the crew, as one of them seemed to justify Darwin's theory of evolution. The student, looking a lot like Cro-Magnon man only left one wondering about his mother. Someone in his family ought to have told him that selling carpets at Allders in Croydon would be more appropriate for him, as no mum in her right mind would let him get his medical paws on her child – no matter what.

The clock clearly stated that it was 12:04, which meant that in about thirty or forty minutes the crew could be in the hospital canteen. What joy!

Two nurses, deep in conversation, approached the chairs occupied by the crew. One was attractive, the other extremely attractive; both rustled slightly.

Boredom and Vultures

'Do you know, who Anthony Rowley was?' asked the attractive nurse.

At this, Luther K was on his feet, and despite the onset of advancing years, still believed that he 'had a way with women'.

A voice from the chairs said, 'Didn't he play in goal for West Brom in the Eighties?'

'What?' said Luther K, annoyed at being interrupted from behind, by his own team.

'He played in goal for West Brom.'

'He most certainly did not!' said Luther K firmly, and then as if wishing to amplify the point, added, '*Heigh ho*, said Rowley.'

'*Heigh ho* said who?'

'Rowley,' said Luther K, desperate to impress.

'*A frog, he would a-wooing go, game on and spinning, Heigh ho, said Rowley…*'

Luther K was grateful for the information supplied by the attractive nurse.

'*Whether his mother would let him or not,*' she continued.

'*With a roly-poly, Heigh ho said Anthony Rowley!*' added Luther K.

'*Gammon and spinach*,' said a voice.

'Gammon and what?' said Luther K, losing momentum.

'*Spinach*,' said the voice, 'It's *gammon and spinach*.'

The staff nurse with the laser eyes had arrived, and Luther K was not about to get into verbal arm wrestling with her.

'It makes more sense… I always thought that "game on and spinning" was something you did when playing darts,' he said, attempting to recover a little ground.

'That's all very well, but who was Anthony Rowley?' enquired the attractive nurse.

'Rowley must have been telling the story,' said Luther K, with the stoop and nod of a second hand car salesman, about to lose his deal of the day.

'And this has nothing to do with a "runcible spoon", does it?' asked the extremely attractive nurse.

'No – that was "The Owl and the Pussycat",' said Luther K in a *I believe I know Edward Lear better than anyone sitting around in A&E at the moment* sort of manner.

'See, I knew it wasn't Anthony Rowley or the frog,' said the

Boredom and Vultures

extremely attractive nurse, and then added, 'what is a runcible spoon?'

'Would someone please stop them!' said a voice in desperation. 'You know he'll only insist on telling us.'

Somebody was heard to say, 'I had a frog once...' But thankfully, nobody was listening.

The clock was at 12:24 (remember the clock?) so it was time for lunch.

On that particular day, the bread and butter pudding with heaps of custard was a winner; both Chris and Keith were seen to be sharing a second helping. This was nothing unusual as they were Yorkshire lads, and puddings – or 'afters' as Keith was known to call them – were a bit of a speciality for the pair of them.

At 16:01 precisely, our consultant started his shift, and told the crew that a lady was being brought in by some members of her family. Nothing unusual about that, but he added that the lady had been found by her daughter, totally unconscious, sitting in a chair, at her home. The lady had been suffering for some years with bowel and respiratory problems, which the hospital had successfully treated. The consultant told them what he found odd was that all the family lived in Stoke, the son and his wife only half a mile from his mother, and not one of them knew she had been ill, or treated in hospital over the past couple of years. Was this of any interest to us?

Jeremy felt we should shoot some footage on this, and interview some of the family. The crew were well pleased at the thought of covering a case, and prepared themselves for the arrival of the lady.

Paramedics wheeled the elderly lady into A&E and five members of her family were taken to a comfortable side room to complete some details for the hospital.

The consultant and two doctors were examining the lady. There wasn't much said. Two nurses familiar to the crew were there, with a sister.

After about forty minutes of very little action but intense examination and concentration, a doctor and the sister left to see the family, who were being cared for by two other nurses and a staff nurse. The consultant and doctor were talking quietly and looking at some charts, one of the nurses was holding the lady's hand.

The consultant turned to the crew and said, 'This lady is 83-years-old and has possibly an hour of her life left, two at the most. Her heart, lungs and kidneys have virtually stopped working, and she should be left quietly, to pass away with peace and dignity. I have to go and explain to the family now.'

Two nurses wheeled the lady to a small room adjacent to A&E where her family could spend a brief time with her.

Jeremy felt, quite rightly, that the lady should be left in peace at the end of her life, with her family, and pulled the vultures back to their chairs.

Just over an hour later, one of the nurses came and told the crew that the lady had passed quietly over to the other side.

It's interesting how peaceful this expression is. Contrast the American hospital, where the crew were filming the previous year. When someone died, it was found incorrect to mention death, but to pass on the information, 'We have negative patient output.'

It had been arranged between Jeremy and the consultant to film an interview with him that evening pending the onslaught of trauma.

By now, the crew knew trauma had a habit of being elsewhere, so the interview with the consultant was a dead cert.

18:22. It must be time to visit the canteen. Chris and Keith were both wondering if any of the bread and butter pudding was left, and would there be some to share. Carlo had received good news that his Italian BMW could be serviced next week. Emma pointed out that Keith's shirts looked a little tired, especially around the collar line, and Jeremy thought his son Sam had the makings of a good seam bowler. This immediately awakened Keith's interest, as he, like Jeremy, was a keen cricket man.

Left to the passions of food, they ate too much, drank lashings of orange juice and coffee, and then went on to cheese things.

Replete, they staggered back to their not so comfy chairs on the outskirts of A&E.

The clock displayed a mean 19:44 and the phone remained quiet.

A nurse rustled past gently, which was pleasant – ephemerally speaking.

Chris mentioned he was going on a couple of charity cycle rides.

Carlo said he was going to Rome to organise the building of a mezzanine floor in his apartment.

Emma thought she and a friend would be going to Mexico later in the year.

Keith told them he had to paint the kitchen.

Emma politely drew attention to the frayed collar on Keith's shirt.

At 20:11 Jeremy returned with news that they were to have a chat with two of the doctors on duty in A&E. Their shift finished at 21:00 and they would be happy to talk on camera about life in A&E – the good points and the pitfalls.

The crew knew this was a good move as only moments with the doctors had been grabbed so far, and here they had a female and a male doctor willing to give Jeremy some good content.

By 22:07 Jeremy was smiling, he now had some positive material on camera from both doctors who were good subjects and willing for Jeremy to use their dialogue anywhere he wished, to tell the story.

Emma arrived with two release forms signed by the doctors, stating they had participated willingly and the information hadn't been extracted from them by torture. She also had four coffees and a cup of very weak tea for the crew – Chris doesn't drink coffee.

They mulled over the content from the doctors and debated whether they should follow the doctors around the following day to make their material more useful, and who knows – they might get a good bit of trauma in A&E while the docs were on shift.

Jeremy decided he would think about it in the morning as it was now pretty late – his watch said it was five minutes to eleven. He said he would go and check with our consultant, who hadn't turned up for his bit of chat, and arrange for a convenient time the following day.

At 23:12 Jeremy returned and said, 'Nothing's happening, let's call it a wrap.'

Boredom and Vultures

They had packed their equipment away, and were passing the night sisters station when the red alert phone rang loudly. Well, it appeared to be loud as everything else was so quiet.

The crew looked at each other. Jeremy said, 'Hang on.'

It was 23:27.

The night sister on the phone was saying, 'Did you say three, plus two from another vehicle?'...pause...'Right, got that, – how long do you think you will be?' she said...pause...

'Okay, twenty to twenty-five minutes.'

She pressed an alarm, which alerted a crash team, and she called our consultant on the intercom. In less than a couple of minutes medical staff of all ranks had arrived in A&E to prepare for the arrivals.

Jeremy turned and said to the crew 'This is the one, let's get ready.' Chris and Keith were half unpacked, and Carlo, as always, was ahead of the game, and had the film magazines loaded in advance.

The consultant was telling Jeremy that a stolen car had been chased by a police car at high speed, the stolen car had crashed, causing the police car to skid and crash into a building. The passenger in the stolen car was seriously injured, and the driver was thought to have a broken leg. Two of the police officers were badly hurt, with the third officer concussed. Paramedics in four ambulances would be arriving with them in about fifteen minutes.

Jeremy was right – this was the one. The crew had waited, and waited; for fifteen days they had waited, and now they were minutes away from unbelievable trauma. As Jeremy said later, 'We had trauma in spades.'

The medical staff were simply – brilliant. A quiet, well-trained urgency, and everything was ready to help the injured.

The passenger from the stolen car was first to arrive. The paramedics thought he was sixteen or seventeen, and had serious injuries to his head, chest and stomach; his left leg was broken. To the crew, he looked terribly injured; his clothing was soaked in blood, as was his head and neck. He was taken quickly into A&E where his clothes were cut from him.

The driver from the stolen car was semiconscious and was taken straight to X-ray.

Paramedics from the two remaining ambulances arrived with the police officers. Two of them were badly injured, and in terrible pain.

The crew returned to the teenager, whose clothes had now been removed. Three nurses and a doctor were cleaning him. The damage to his body now appeared more obvious, but the consultant was more concerned about internal injuries, and within minutes the stomach was opened allowing thorough checks for internal bleeding to take place.

Jeremy timed his questions to the consultant with perfection, who explained exactly what he was doing and why.

Other doctors and medical staff were already attending to the police officers, who fortunately didn't have serious internal injuries, but did have an assortment of broken bones.

A mobile X-ray unit arrived in A&E, so we all pulled out while the youth was being checked for damaged bones.

This was a ten-minute break for Chris and Carlo to check the camera gate for any hairs which might have crept in during the scramble. As usual the gate was clear; both Chris and Carlo have always kept the camera equipment in mint condition. While assisting Chris on camera, Carlo was also assisting Keith by supplying him with fresh rolls of tape, and taking the recorded ones for safe keeping. It was a well-tried system they had perfected on other hospital shoots, and now was being pushed to the limit.

The X-ray unit moved away, and it was decided to give the teenager a CT scan. The Scan Unit was already waiting for the entourage from A&E when they arrived. The crew were allowed to film all that was happening in every department, which made working a lot easier when filming difficult subjects.

The scan was under way when the consultant, who did have a wry sense of humour, was heard to say in the darkness of the room, 'Do you think his brain looked like that before the accident?'

Back in A&E, the police had been heavily sedated to ease the pain, and Chris was collecting useful footage of anything that moved, or didn't, come to think of it. Keith was attempting to record some stereo sound of A&E, which could be converted into

NICAM for the Channel 4 viewer who had the facilities to enjoy the spectrum. Carlo and Emma were like solid rock, giving the crew the full support they required. Jeremy steered the unit with impressive professional calm. The reliable thing about Jeremy is that he always has his brain in the right gear in these situations, particularly when asking questions.

The consultant was back in A&E still performing minor surgery, the nursing staff still performing minor miracles, and still smiling to encourage the crew.

It was 04:23 when Jeremy asked the consultant what the outcome of the surgery was.

'If I hadn't opened the boy up when I did, and stem the internal bleeding at the aorta in the first half hour, its likely he would not have made it to the morning. The CT scan has shown some damage to the brain, but I don't know if that was there before the accident. His friend, the driver, has a broken leg, which has been set, and he'll wake up with a headache.

'The police were quite fortunate for such a bad crash. X-rays have shown quite a few broken bones, but in a couple of months the two of them will be moving around again, and the other one should be out in two or three days.'

Jeremy and the crew filmed and chatted to some of doctors and nurses recording their reactions to the events, and amazingly, by the time the crew had wrapped up their equipment at 05:14 the A&E Department was spotless, all the beds with clean sheets, and not a drop of blood anywhere. Every surface totally clean, with no hint of the bloody drama that had unfolded at midnight.

These people are not just doctors and nurses, that they most certainly are, but they are also special, remarkable people whose true worth can never be measured.

The crew didn't rise much before lunch, and over the meal had a complete debriefing on the drama they had been part of the previous night. Two hours of film and sound had been shot, and Jeremy knew the content was exactly what Channel 4 needed, but the big question was how to get clearance from the family of the teenager who was lying in intensive care at Stoke Hospital. What kind of parent would want their son to be seen by the nation in the state he was last night?

When the crew arrived at the hospital Jeremy was informed that the parents of the teenager were in intensive care, and understood that their son had been filmed for television the previous night. Jeremy and Emma went to see the parents, expecting only the worst. Now, both of them are excellent diplomats and the crew knew they would put up a good case.

The parents were introduced to Jeremy and Emma who explained why they were making a film in that particular hospital.

The reaction of the parents was totally unexpected. They were pleased a film was being made, as it had been explained to them that their son probably wouldn't be alive now had the consultant not operated immediately, and it had been filmed for the nation to see, but also, and more important, for their son to see.

This was not the first time he had stolen a car and been involved with the police, so they would be glad to be interviewed by Jeremy, and would sign a release form with pleasure, if this was a chance of bringing their son to his senses.

Jeremy and Emma realised they had both just discovered gold.

The programme went out to rave reviews. Channel 4 was pleased, which augured well for a future commission. Jeremy and Emma were pleased, the consultant and the A&E staff thought it was good, Chris 'the cameraman', ever faithful to his Quaker school, felt it 'may or may not' be representative of the hospital. Carlo and Luther K thought they had done okay – and nobody consulted the fly on the wall.

NB   Four weeks after the shoot, Jeremy and Emma bought Keith a brand new shirt from GAP, which was, without any debate, the best shirt he had ever worn.

The Search for Lord Lucan

In 1994, it had been twenty years since the disappearance of Lord Lucan, and the horrifying murder of Sandra Rivett at the Lucan family home in Belgravia. Channel Four Television decided to make a programme to cover the investigation so far, and was fortunate to have Detective Chief Superintendent Roy Ranson as advisor. He was the senior officer who led the Scotland Yard inquiry at the time of the murder.

Channel Four was wise enough in commissioning Susanna White to direct the film, which suited me to a T. I had worked with Susanna on four of her previous films, and we got on well. She told me the film would be shot in Belgravia, at one or two locations coinciding with Lucan's last known sightings, and on a trip to Botswana, where some believed he was living.

I had forgotten a lot of the detail relating to the crime, but once we started shooting it came flooding back.

Lord Lucan was estranged from Lady Lucan and legal activity was under way over custody of the children. A live-in nanny, Sandra Rivett, had been employed, and found to be most satisfactory. Lady Lucan and Sandra soon became on first name terms, and the children appeared to be at ease in her company.

People who knew them commented on the similarity between them. They were both 5 feet 2 inches tall, of similar build with almost the same hairstyle.

On the evening of the murder, Thursday, 7 November 1974, Lord Lucan let himself into the house somewhere around 8:30 p.m. His eldest daughter had told him, a week or so earlier, that Thursday was the nanny's day off. He had with him a large canvas mailbag, and a length of lead pipe covered in surgical tape. Lady Lucan was upstairs watching television with her eldest child. Unknown to Lucan, Sandra Rivett was resting in her room recovering from an illness. At about nine o'clock, it is thought, she decided to go down to the kitchen to make some tea for Lady Lucan, as she normally had a drink at that time of the evening.

When she got to the stairs that lead to the basement, she must have remembered the reason it was dark was due to the light bulb which had blown a few days earlier, and neither she nor Lady Lucan were tall enough to replace it. It was then that she was brutally attacked, and murdered.

After about twenty minutes Lady Lucan wondered why the tea was taking so long, and went downstairs to find Sandra. She called out Sandra's name and got no reply. Lucan must have thought he was going crazy, to hear his wife's voice calling for Sandra, when he knew he had just killed his wife. It was at this moment that Lucan attacked Lady Lucan with the lead pipe, already covered in Sandra's blood. Lady Lucan fell to the floor screaming, where she was struck again and again. After kicking and struggling for her life, she managed to crawl backwards through his legs, reach up and grab his genitals with all her strength. He apparently dropped the lead pipe and fell back against the wall.

Lady Lucan managed to get out of the house, stagger down the road to the Plumbers Arms on the corner, where she collapsed, and the landlord and bar staff sent for the police.

By the time Detective Chief Superintendent Roy Ranson and his colleagues got to the pub, the ambulance had already taken Lady Lucan to the hospital, and the local police had discovered the body of Sandra Rivett in the basement of the house.

Lord Lucan's next move was to drive to Uckfield, West Sussex, in a borrowed Ford Corsair, to call on his close friends, the Maxwell-Scotts. He asked Susan Maxwell-Scott if he could have some writing paper, which she naturally gave him, along with a whisky. He then wrote two letters to his brother-in-law, William Shand-Kydd: one giving his version of what had happened that evening, and the other asking Shand-Kydd to organise the distribution of the proceeds from an auction to go to the major creditors he was in debt to. He closed the letter saying that 'the other creditors can get lost for the time being'.

At the time of the murder, it was estimated that the gambling debts of Lord Lucan had amounted to some £50,000 – and his friends called him Lucky!

Lucan left Susan Maxwell-Scott at 1:15 a.m. and that was the last time he was seen in Britain.

Early the next morning, the police in Newhaven on the Sussex coast contacted Scotland Yard to inform them they had found the Ford Corsair, which Lucan had been driving. There was blood on the driver's seat, and the boot contained a length of lead pipe wrapped in surgical tape, plus a bottle of vodka, Lord Lucan's favourite tipple.

Almost twenty years later Roy Ranson told me in Botswana, that it still puzzled him as to why the Maxwell-Scotts had not reported any of this to Scotland Yard the following day: 'Little things like Lord Lucan arriving at their house at about 11:30 in the evening, driving a Ford Corsair, which wasn't his, having blood on his usually immaculate clothes, writing two letters which we posted for him the following day, and after having a couple of whiskies, driving off into the night,' Roy recalled with a tired smile of twenty years. The news had, after all, been on every bulletin on TV, radio, and was headlines in every paper throughout Britain that day.

At a later date Susan Maxwell-Scott had written a letter to the *Daily Star* justifying her loyalty to Lord Lucan. She remarked that 'friends have loyalty to each other, if not, they are mere acquaintances not friends. Loyalty among friends is the highest morality in life'.

I wonder how convincing that was to the family of Sandra Rivett? As someone said, 'Poor Sandra lost her life because she just happened to be the same height and shape as Lady Lucan, had a similar hair style, and neither of them were tall enough to change a light bulb.'

Our filming started in Belgravia at a house identical to that of Lord and Lady Lucan. It had been decided by Susanna and Channel Four that we would dramatise the murder, using actors, and be advised by Roy Ranson, as to the accuracy of our efforts.

Chris Morphet, 'the cameraman', and Carlo, his assistant, had been invited to shoot the drama/documentary on film, and not video (oh deepest joy). This was to be real movie-making!

On day one, instead of the normal crew of four, there were at least a dozen people attending to details of hair, costumes, make up, lashings of 'Kensington Gore' (stage blood), and we actually had actors, who were lovely people. Why should I be surprised?

About 9:30 a.m., ex-Detective Chief Superintendent Roy Ranson arrived, and was introduced to each of the crew. He had retired from the Metropolitan Police, and then worked for the BBC as Chief Investigator. Corruption and theft were predominant activities at that time in the Nations favourite Corporation.

I liked him immediately, and we seemed to build up a good relationship, which was beneficial to both of us, as we were to share a room at the Mashatu Game Reserve in Botswana the following month.

During the next fortnight, we completed the dramatisation, and shot sequences in Uckfield, Newhaven, and a small airfield near Brighton, where we were told how easy it is for someone to leave the country in a light aircraft, the passengers totally unidentified.

We interviewed Charles Benson, Lord Lucan's Old Etonian school friend, at Newmarket racecourse. He was the racing tipster for the *Daily Express* known as 'The Scout'. He proved to be charming, as one would have expected, and gave a good account of his involvement with Lucan in 1974 to Roy Ranson. This was nothing new to Roy, but it was to us; in fact all the friends and acquaintances of Lord and Lady Lucan were courteous, and helpful as far as a 20-year memory would allow.

Lord Lucan's favourite club, the Clermont in Belgrave Square, gave us open house to film interviews at the club, and also to shoot sequences around the gaming tables when the club was closed. It was here we were shown Lord Lucan's personal chips, marked with 'LL' for Lucky Lucan. I believe the highest value of a chip was £5,000, the lowest coming in at £100. This was a gambling man with clout, but unfortunately not too much 'luck'!

After interviewing all loyal and compliant members of the Lucan set we were allowed to, it was not too surprising to discover that 'quite naturally' they knew nothing of his whereabouts, or even if he should be still alive. After all it was twenty years without any contact – supposedly even with his children.

All through this time Roy Ranson smiled gently, he was

hearing nothing new. He admitted he was impressed that, after this length of time, the Lucan pack were still holding together. As yet the cracks were not showing.

The situation in Botswana, however, was completely different. There had been many sightings and confirmations of Lord Lucan's existence from a wide variety of people, and they were willing to talk on camera.

Chris Morphet 'the cameraman' was unable to come with us to Botswana. I can't remember the exact reason, but I expect Spurs had a home game. Carlo wouldn't be coming with us, either. The cameraman assigned to the job in Botswana was Mike Eley, and his assistant Luke Hallam. I'd heard plenty about Mike, but not Luke. Mike was rated in the top five documentary cameramen at the time (and still is), so I was looking forward to working with him quite a lot.

We all met at Heathrow for the flight to Johannesburg.

What no one had told me was Mike and Luke were probably the best-looking chaps on the documentary circuit, as Roy Ranson said to me, 'Where did they get these two from – Central Casting? I've arrested people for being that good looking.'

'I don't know – but they are in the first division, and they have one ace track record.' I replied.

It was a good flight to Johannesburg, and we enjoyed our time getting acquainted.

'Baggage Claim' always takes a while for a crew, as we often have an assortment of twenty to thirty metal boxes and cases, especially for two weeks in unknown territory. We had got all the crew boxes and bits off the carousel in about half an hour, which is pretty good for British Airways. The only item missing was Roy Ranson's suitcase. We stood waiting for some five minutes when someone remarked that the large solitary suitcase going round the carousel had passed us four or five times. On its next lap, as the case came up to us, Susanna said to Roy, 'Isn't that your case?' Looking more closely, Roy replied with embarrassment, 'Yes – it is,' and took the missing case from the carousel. A voice behind was heard to say, 'Lucan, – you're quite safe.' Roy smiled.

We were met at the airport by Clive Stafford, our South African 'fixer' – it's essential for any film crew to have a local 'fixer' on board who understands the language, the customs, the driving habits, and the money. These people can also walk up a tree barefoot, kill a deadly snake with their bare hands, and stay alive for days just eating maggots and frogs. Clive was such a chap.

A rather unusual plane had been chartered for us to fly from Johannesburg to Gaborone in Botswana. If the seating arrangements had been that of a traditional aircraft it would probably have seated twenty-five to thirty passengers, but this one was fitted with three sofas, four armchairs facing each other, and a couple of smaller easy chairs. The 'usual offices' were so vast that one could bend down to tie ones shoe laces without fear of being wedged there for life. This was flying Luxury Class.

We checked in to the Gaborone Sun Hotel, which was to be our base for the next few days. It had changed its name from the Holiday Inn Hotel some seven or eight years previously. It was also the location of some of the sightings of Lord Lucan. This certainly added an air of adventure to the job in the hope that we too would be able to spot him!

The following day Roy Ranson met up with Russell Allen, an ex-Detective Superintendent of the Fraud Squad, and old colleague from Scotland Yard, who was assisting the local police in setting up an anti-corruption unit.

We filmed a sequence with the two of them chatting and looking at maps showing the Tuli Block, a vast area on the border of Botswana and South Africa. The Limpopo River ran along the border of the two countries for many hundreds of miles. The border controls were often only open between 8 a.m. and 4 a.m., and many of these manned by just a couple of policemen. We were told that in the dry season it was possible to cross wherever you wished in the shallow water. Russell told Roy that the Tuli Block was the home to many very wealthy white families who lived on huge farming estates and game reserves. Most of these estates were the size of Surrey, some even larger, and all of them were surrounded by high fencing and formidable gates, with security guards.

The houses these families lived in were built some fifteen to twenty miles or so from the gates, and the drive could take up to two hours, as the so-called roads were rough tracks, through dried-up river-beds, hardly designed for horses, let alone vehicles.

Russell also pointed out to us that if you wanted to disappear, Botswana had to be one of the best places you could choose. The total area of Botswana is greater than France, but only has a population of Croydon and Tooting.

When we got back to our hotel that evening, a Botswanan man was waiting to see Roy. We had only been there a couple of days, but the word was out. Roy told us that the man was called 'Brumpy' (I think that's what he said), and that the man had information on Lord Lucan, but he wanted paying for it. After some negotiations between Susanna, 'Brumpy', Clive and Roy, a deal was agreed. 'Brumpy' told us he had seen Lucan gambling in the very casino of the hotel we were sitting in.

He did say that Lord Lucan had been seen in Bulawayo in Zimbabwe, but couldn't give any details. This news wasn't particularly earth-moving, as Roy pointed out to us – the Lucan family farm was only a few miles north-west of Bulawayo, and if Lucan was in the area, its quite probable he would have visited his relatives on the farm, and could have called in at Bulawayo.

The following day, arrangements were made to fly to the Mashatu Game Reserve, and visit the Tuli Block.

It wasn't a long flight from Gaborone to the Tuli Lodge private airstrip, and on landing it became immediately obvious how easy it would be for anyone to disappear. The airstrip had one hut at the end of the runway, with a small sign which indicated that this was Tuli Lodge Customs Control and Immigration. There was nobody manning the post.

Mashatu Game Reserve was stunning, with ostriches, zebras, elephants and a multitude of gloriously coloured birds surrounding us. As I mentioned, Roy and I had formed a good working and friendly relationship, so it was of no inconvenience to share a rondavel with him. From the outside the rondavel looked like a simple round white building with a conical straw roof, and two simple square windows either side of the door, which was also simple. On entering the room, it took on the characteristics of a 'Tardis': everything seemed bigger. The room contained two big single beds with fitted mosquito nets, two large wardrobes, a sofa, a dressing table, and two doors. One led to a large bathroom and toilet, and the other to a storage area. When you went outside and looked back at the building, you knew it was impossible for all that to fit inside the building you had just left. I thought, Well, this is Africa, and when I returned to the rondavel, everything fitted perfectly fine.

Strange – this African thing!

That evening, while we were getting ready to meet the others for dinner, Roy told me a convincing account of one of the sightings.

He said that in 1977, three years after the murder of Sandra Rivett, he visited a man in Leeds Prison who, like Lucan, had fled the country to avoid a prison sentence.

My thought then was – Why was Roy visiting him in a Leeds prison?

The man's name was Trevor Walton, and when he fled the country, he went to South Africa, and joined the Rhodesian Army. It was a habit of soldiers on leave to travel to Gaborone in Botswana and stay at the Holiday Inn Hotel. The hotel had all the facilities a soldier could require – gambling – alcohol – and girls.

During the first evening at the bar, Trevor Walton was chatting to a white man from a Botswanan Construction Company. They were talking about South Africa, politics and the 'oddballs' that turned up there: 'Take Lord Lucan, for instance, at the bar over there,' he said, pointing a man out to Trevor.

The man was over six feet tall with dark hair combed back at a slight angle, and probably about forty-years-old. His bearing was very upright, and Walton thought almost military. Trevor Walton told Roy he had seen the same man later on, playing craps in the casino, and that he had heard him speaking to someone in what Walton described as a posh English accent. After asking around Walton was told that the man lived in Palapye, a town not far away, and he had something to do with mining.

Roy showed Walton some photographs of Lucan taken in 1973, and Walton said, without any doubt, that the man he saw was the man in the photographs.

I thought this was gripping stuff, and asked Roy if there had been any follow-up.

This was just another story of another sighting told to him by a man in a Leeds jail. No solid evidence, and Lucan's gambling appeared to centre on card games, and roulette at the Clermont Club, not crap tables.

Some time later, however, Roy discovered that in the months leading up to the murder, Lucan had got hooked on shooting craps at a club other than the Clermont. Trevor Walton could never have known this.

Roy told me that this had triggered his interest in Trevor Walton again, and he remembered that Walton had also given him a lot more information about his leave in Botswana.

He had said that the town was crowded, due to a rugby match between South Africa and the All Blacks, which South Africa won.

Roy said he checked all the details, and found Trevor Walton's story to be absolutely true. Scotland Yard contacted the police in Botswana, and asked them to check out the town of Palapye, and the whereabouts of a mining office from which Lucan might be operating, and the frequency of Lucan's gambling visits at the Holiday Inn Casino.

'No inquiries were made,' said Roy.

Early next morning we headed for the Tuli Block. It was about a four-hour drive in open vehicles through some breathtaking scenery.

Arrangements had been made through a couple of journalists in Johannesburg to visit one of the farms, and to film the owner about a sighting of Lord Lucan some eighteen years earlier when he visited this particular farm.

The gates to the estate were not only high and covered in razor wire, but also very heavily guarded. Susanna and Clive offered our paperwork and permits to a senior guard, and amazingly the gates opened. As we drove through, a large fuse box with a lightning symbol and '6,000 Volts' marked on it was spotted at the side of the fence, with heavy-duty wiring connecting it to the gates and the fence.

'Do you think they have something to hide?' said someone.

The drive to the house was about an hour, where we were met by three very healthy large dogs. We decided not to get out of the vehicle. Some black houseboys came out of the house and called to the dogs who left us immediately.

The owner of the farm arrived from the house, and welcomed us in a polite English accent. Tea and coffee were brought out to us, while Mike, Luke and myself unloaded the gear and prepared to shoot the interview.

'He's had second thoughts and decided not to do it,' said Susanna, in a low voice. Clive was talking to the man with Roy looking on, and we just watched from a distance.

With diplomacy and courtesy to the fore, Susanna walked back to the group to attempt another line of persuasion.

After a few minutes of polite exchange, the owner informed us that not only was he not going to give us an interview, he did not know Lord Lucan, and Lucan had never been to the farm eighteen years ago.

We packed and left.

Back at Mashatu Game Reserve that evening, over dinner, Roy told all of us that the negative reception we had received that day was typical of those he had previously encountered. Journalists who had made enquiries in the past about Lord Lucan, and his possible links with the Tuli Block, were often told firmly that 'it would be better they should leave the country.'

I forget who, but someone had told Susanna of a woman named Janice Main, who had a positive sighting of Lucan in the late Seventies. She had a crocodile farm on the outskirts of the Okavango Delta in the north west of Botswana, and we planned to visit her the following day.

We flew up to a town called Maim, and drove some distance to the farm on the edge of the delta. Janice Main was an attractive, intelligent woman, who remembered very clearly the events of her sighting of Lord Lucan. The ingredient, which made her particularly attractive to us, was her wish to tell us her story on camera.

In 1977, Janice was in Gaborone. It was a particularly quiet Saturday afternoon, and she decided to visit the hairdresser's. The salon she used was on the ground floor of a large office block called Debswana House. She told us the only reason she mentioned this was that de Beers, the diamond merchants sorted their diamonds in offices on the top floor, and rumour had it that Lucan was involved in mining diamonds.

As she left the hairdresser's it was still very quiet and therefore very easy to hear someone walking behind her. She had not walked far before she noticed very positive footsteps on the marble floor coming from behind. The steps were so precise she said that she instinctively turned round, and found she was looking straight into the face of Lord Lucan who was walking towards her. She told us she was stunned; various people and journalists had been looking for him all over the Tuli Block, and here she was looking him in the face.

She said she was so shocked that she turned around and pretended to look into another window for something. As he went past, she got another good look at him, only to confirm her initial reaction.

She described him as being of early middle age, of military bearing, and good posture. She followed him out of Debswana House to the car park where he got into a Toyota Land Cruiser and drove off.

She knew beyond any shadow of doubt that she had seen Lord Lucan.

She was good; she was very, very good. We had a convincing story, told to us by a convincing lady, and we had it on film.

Susanna was pleased!

As we flew back to Johannesburg the next day, one of the questions being asked was, 'Is Lucan in Botswana or not?'

We all seemed split in our opinions, but I do remember being the only one adamant or rash enough to suggest that I believed Lucan was still alive, and living in Botswana. Roy was not sure as he didn't have any hard evidence, but said he thought he could be persuaded.

Susannah said, 'she was open to suggestion that he was there'.

After a couple of days shooting some interviews with two journalists in Johannesburg about other reported sightings, and still coming to no further conclusions, we flew back to London.

The film was well received, and Susanna was pleased with the good reviews. I think my family ended up being uncertain, with the older ones saying Lucan was a 'goner' and the younger members feeling quite strongly that he was either in the Tuli Block, or living on the family farm in Zimbabwe.

January 2002

Susanna was having dinner with some friends in Notting Hill. There were seven or eight people around the table, four of whom she had not previously met.

During the evening the chat got around to various topics – politics, the press, travel, and one of the men mentioned he had lived in Botswana for many years. Susanna asked him what part of the country he had lived in, and his reply quite startled her.

'The Tuli Block,' he said.

She told him that she had worked in Botswana in 1994, and had visited the Tuli Block.

'Why were you in that area?' asked the man.

'We were making a documentary film about Lord Lucan,' she said.

'Did you visit Lucan at his house?' he asked.

Susanna just stared at him looking totally dumbfounded and said 'You mean he actually lived there?'

'Yes, he lived on the next farm but one to ours, he died a couple of years ago.'

This news was almost beyond belief for Susanna, but then she remembered that about two years previously she had read in the press that as Lord Lucan had been missing for twenty-five years, his son, Lord George Bingham, would now legally become the new Lord Lucan.

If what she had been told was true, and if the report in the papers of two years ago, which coincided with what the dinner guest had told her, was correct, then a line could be drawn under the search.

Sadly, having died two years after our return from Botswana, ex-Detective Chief Superintendent Roy Ranson never knew just how close he had come to finding 'Lucky' Lucan.

The Director – the PA – and the Tick

A doctor in Ealing Hospital told me, that cellulitis always attacked the weaker parts of the anatomy, especially where circulation is poor. In 1965 the main veins in my legs had been stripped to clear the varicose ulcers on my ankles (a genetic gift from birth). In 1989 therefore it was not surprising to be the owner of a right leg and ankle which appeared almost twice the size of normal, and had turned a sort of blotchy brown with purple tram lines. This condition was compounded by a running temperature of 103°.

The doctor said, 'Not to worry, you'll be up and about in a week, just take it easy with the tap-dancing.'

This was all very well for the doctor, but about three weeks earlier Sarah Cunliffe, a director I had worked with before, had phoned to ask if I would like to go with her crew to the rainforests in northern Thailand. The film she had planned was to record the singing apes at Khao Yai.

Naturally, I had agreed. For me this was like having gold dropped right into your lap. I always enjoyed working with Sarah, and filming wildlife in Thailand was a must.

A possible week in a hospital bed, hot and sweaty, with the blood being shampooed by an intravenous drip, did not augur well for a trip to Thailand in ten days time.

As promised by the medic, I was out of hospital the following week with a leg looking more of a reasonable match to the other one, except for a few blotches and a definite reluctance to perform as a leg. 'Nothing to worry about,' I had been told at the hospital, 'keep exercising the leg.'

I phoned Sarah and told her about the offending limb, as I didn't wish to be a burden to the crew. Sarah, whose husband was a doctor, told me she felt certain that in a week's time all would be fine, with all my bits working properly. She was looking forward to the trip.

By the time Sarah and I met at Heathrow the leg was nearly back to normal. We were to fly out together as James the

The Director – the PA – and the Tick

cameraman and the rest of the unit were already in Thailand. Sarah had thoughtfully booked seats on the 747 with plenty of legroom so I wouldn't be cramped. What we hadn't prepared for was the effect of flying at high altitude under cabin pressure. Consequently, by the time we arrived at Bangkok the leg was a similar shape to what it had been in hospital.

We were met at Bangkok by Sarah's assistant, Jane-Marie, who sorted out the customs details covering my sound equipment. The Thai customs seemed friendly but puzzled to see a baggage trolley with me perched on top and one leg in the air. Sarah, who was pushing the trolley was thinking, Oh my god, I've got a right one here, and I was thinking, How incredibly humiliating – this has to be the most preposterous entry into Bangkok.

As soon as we arrived at the hotel, Sarah was on the phone to her husband, who prescribed 'compression and elevation' as the best remedy.

Sarah and Jane-Marie, who were never known to stand on ceremony, left me in my room, laying on my bed with both legs (one blotchy, one not) elevated on some metal cases and a couple of pillows. They were off to buy crêpe bandages, liniment, and oil to keep the skin lubricated. I pointed out that it was late and asked, 'Is it safe? Will the pharmacies be open?'

Sarah grinned and reminded me, 'This is Bangkok, you can get anything, anywhere, anytime.' She also mentioned she had to buy underpants for James and the crew, already up at Khao Yai.

I thought, Underpants for James, I must have misheard – well whatever!

About half an hour passed when there was a knock on the door. The door opened, and a lady of oriental origin asked me if I required any room service. I told her not at the moment, she smiled politely, turned to close the door, and then turned back as if to say something, but again just smiled at the European male, laying flat on his back in his underpants and shirt, with his legs in the air being supported by metal boxes and two pillows. Still smiling, she turned and closed the door.

As promised, Sarah and Jane-Marie returned with bandages, liniment and lubricating oil. Sarah began to administer the remedy suggested by her husband. Legs had been oiled, nothing

The Director – the PA – and the Tick

was left to chance, some liniment strips placed around ankles, and crêpe bandages were being strapped firmly around the legs, when there was a knock at the door.

I ought to have mentioned before, Sarah was a lovely healthy, young woman of about thirty. Jane-Marie was similarly a young woman of about twenty-five or six. Both could be described as Chris Morphet 'the cameraman' was once heard to say, 'drop-dead gorgeous.'

The lady of oriental origin, who had visited earlier, had returned with an oriental friend to have a look at this unusual man in only his underpants and shirt, with his legs (one blotchy, one not) up in the air.

They naturally never expected to see two gorgeous European ladies in attendance, oiling and strapping the raised limbs. This man was getting a form of room service seldom seen in Bangkok, and they closed the door giggling.

After two days of sorting out permits, transport and the like, my legs were responding to the elevation and compression satisfactorily, so Sarah decided that the following day we would head north for the rainforest.

In Bangkok there are no traffic jams – Bangkok *is* a traffic jam. After nearly three hours we made the outskirts of the city. It was immense relief to reach the rainforest and the Rangers' lodge some hours later.

The crew were there to meet us, and helped to unload the vehicle, which always endears them to one instantly.

James Gray, the cameraman, who I had only heard about but never met, proved to be a fellow well met. James was not only an experienced wildlife cameraman in the Premier League, but also a film-maker who had made the photography of sub-miniature insects his forte – and he was good! Added to this he was a Doctor of Psychology and a jolly splendid all-round chap. It may not be apparent, but I did become a fan of his very rapidly!

The first morning I was woken up at 4 a.m. by a most strange sound in the distance, which echoed slightly through the forest. It was strange but was also quite beautiful. I couldn't imagine what it might be. I thought it might be a large bird as it sounded too clear to be an animal. The call, which seemed to be a mile or so away, lasted about a minute and then a silence, apart from other gentle sounds as the forest awakened. After no more than ten or fifteen seconds there was another call, which sounded similar, but appeared to come from the opposite direction. Again, this was from a considerable distance. I thought, This is crazy – no bird could finish calling and then fly at least two miles in ten seconds and start calling again! I was still pondering when there was another call from another direction, and again from a considerable way off.

By 4:30 a.m. the forest was filled with such stunning birdsong and calls from animals you would find hard to imagine. It only has to be heard for a few moments, and you remember why you always say 'yes' to work in the rainforest!

We were all up at 5 o'clock getting ready for our first trek to find the 'singing apes', and I told James about the incredible bird calls that started around 4 a.m., and then again a few seconds later from elsewhere.

He smiled. 'Those were the apes – isn't it a beautiful sound?'

'Those were the apes!' I mouthed.

James nodded. 'All you have to do is to record them in your best stereo while I am filming them. Get a synchronising mark on camera and sound, and we can all go home.'

'If we can get nearer to them, I can get some stunning recordings of them, surrounded with wonderful forest atmosphere,' I enthused.

'Oh, we can get close to them alright,' said James, 'we just can't see them. This is a good time to be here as they are active and moving around in the canopy, but it's the end of the rainy season and the foliage in the canopy is lush and quite dense. That's where the apes like to be, eighty to ninety feet above us, that's why we can't see them – but you can hear them.'

'How do they move so quickly?' I asked James.

'They don't move that quickly,' he replied, 'they are territorial and sing to let the other families of apes around them know that they are still there and haven't moved on, and then the other apes reply, that's why they sound similar, but from opposite directions.'

We left our base about 5:30 and headed for the nearest camera hide. This was roughly forty-five minutes walk through dense forest, and involved climbing down some quite steep muddy slopes and up the other side. The crew had shown me great kindness by carrying all of my sound equipment, and leaving me with just myself to look after.

My plan was to always keep one of them in my sight, or at least to be able to hear them. My reasoning was, that way I wouldn't get lost.

What I hadn't reckoned on was the fitness of the healthy young crew, who had been there for a week already, and were used to the muddy slopes of the rainforest. Also, they knew the way. I hadn't appreciated the amount of noise in the forest at that time of day. Any chatting in front of me was completely masked by hornbills, singing apes and parrots, glorious birdsong and, as far as I was concerned, what sounded like some creatures of unknown origin.

About fifty minutes into the trek, climbing over many a huge tree buttress, and working my way through lianas hanging from the canopy – I stopped – I listened. I listened some more – no voices could be heard, and I could see no member of the crew in front or behind me. The forest sounded spacious and wonderful. I listened again – I knew I was lost.

After a few moments of more listening, I called out, 'Hello!'

The forest replied at its glorious best.

I called again.

The creatures of the forest continued their beautiful chorus.

I decided after some time that 'Hello' shouted in an *I'm so sorry to trouble you* manner, was probably of little value in my predicament. Something a bit more aggressive and longer was required.

'Can anyone hear me?' I yelled, and waited. 'Is anybody there?'

Ten minutes must have passed when I began to wonder how far away the others were. They had told me it was only about forty-five minutes to the first location, but then that was probably timing estimated by those in the peak of fitness (and they were fit). If a unit was towing a damaged crew member approaching the springtime of his senility, then the drag factor would be noticeable.

The Director – the PA – and the Tick

It was now over an hour since we left base and this crew member was standing alone in a rainforest shouting, 'Hello!'

'Do not move, stay where you are!' shouted a voice with a foreign accent.

I didn't move.

'Shout again please,' yelled the voice.

'Hello – I'm over here!' I called, and then added, 'over here by the big tree.' I cannot believe I said that. If one was about to introduce the oxymoron, I had succeeded. The rainforest looks the same which ever way 'over here' is.

'Shout again!' called the man.

I did, and within a minute a forest ranger had found me. With a huge grin on his face he told me it was this way. I wasn't concerned with which way, I was only too pleased to have been found. The rest of the crew were only five minutes away, and the apes, although still singing, had left.

The Rangers had built a camera platform in an area of the canopy known to be inhabited by apes. After three days with no success we moved on. The lush foliage was so dense, James and his best lens simply couldn't see them.

During one of our lulls in ape-spotting, Jane-Marie advised me to tuck my trousers into my socks. As it was the end of the rains, the leeches and ticks were at their most active, and just loved crawling up the hairs on European male legs and setting up lodgings in the warm hairy bits for a jolly good binge. She also gave me a can of repellent spray for my socks and ankles, and crêpe bandages, which she assured me was the best deterrent in town, or out of it.

When we got back to our lodge, I stripped off down to my underwear to check on any new arrivals. Jane-Marie was absolutely right; I had collected about half a dozen leeches on my right ankle, which had now swollen to the size of a small football. The swelling was not due to the leeches, but to the walking and standing throughout the day. Two ticks were struggling up the hairs on my thigh to gain higher altitude and the warmth of unknown hairy regions. I decided there and then that I would not sleep without wearing the tightest underpants I had, and also spray them with the best deterrent in town. I'd managed to remove

The Director – the PA – and the Tick

the newcomers and was examining my ankle when the door opened and one of the crew came in to deposit some camera gear.

The lodge was built from timber throughout, and my room contained ten single mattresses, each on its own platform, which ran the length of one wall. The other long wall contained wardrobes and store cupboards for whatever. This room was all mine, except it was also used by the crew as a base for some camera equipment, as well as for my sound gear.

The crew member noticed my ankle, thought it looked a bit of a mess, and just happened to mention to Sarah that I had 'an ankle Homer Simpson would be proud of'.

Within five minutes Sarah had come to my room with cream, oil and fresh bandages. She took a small metal camera case, covered it with a towel, told me to put my leg on it, and started to massage the oil into my ankle. This she continued to do for about twenty minutes, and when I say massage, I mean firm powerful massage. This caused some pain, but I could tell Sarah was rubbing with intent, and the ultimate effect was of healing. I didn't know what she was doing, but I did trust her.

When the massage was finished, she strapped the leg and ankle firmly with the new crêpe bandage, and told me to stay on the bed with the leg elevated. I was not going to argue.

This was way beyond the call of duty, and I pointed out that this wasn't in her contract, though I was immensely grateful to her and her healing powers. I argued that I was able to rub my legs with the oil, after all she had just completed a long day from 4:30 a.m., walking through pretty dense rain forest, and carrying more camera gear than ever expected. She had also repeated the effort on the return journey back to base. Sarah pointed out to me, quite clearly, that it mattered not what was in her contract, her neck was on the line to take back to Blighty, film footage of singing apes, with digital stereo sound which was totally synchronised to the picture, and although we hadn't got it yet, when those apes appeared in camera range, singing their hearts out, she wanted me mobile and up and at 'em, and if she had to go through the rubbing routine every day to get it, she would.

'Furthermore, you are a man, and you wouldn't rub hard enough, because of the pain. Okay?'

She continued with this treatment for the next twelve days, until the swelling had disappeared.

I thought, Sarah, you are a remarkable lady.

Over the next two weeks, the singing apes were heard clearly every day, but we only got glimpses of them. Usually, by the time we had seen them and got the camera set up, they had gone, singing happily as they went.

It was about the middle of the third week, and we were driving along a road high in the rainforest. The hillside sloped away at one side quite steeply, and we were able to look down on to the canopy of the forest. It was around 10:30 a.m., a time when the forest began to quieten down.

We came round a slight curve in the road, and almost immediately spotted a solitary ape singing loudly to some distant colleague in the next territory. The ape was in clear view, about 200 feet below us, and swinging from a branch. James and the rest of us were out of the vehicle, and climbing down the slope with the basic camera and sound gear, trying not to scare the operatic ape. Everything appeared to be working our way. We were now about level with the ape 100 metres from it. James thought that was close enough; any closer and it might disappear. The camera was fitted with a monster lens. Jane-Marie helped me to set up the stereo microphones, and James gave us thumbs up. The shot he had was a good head and shoulders of the ape who was still singing to his next-door neighbour, and the neighbour replying obligingly. I was willing the apes next door to keep going, as this would hopefully encourage our potential star to do his best for the camera by replying.

After twenty minutes he must have had enough of the movie business, and moved off quietly. As James said, 'He's probably going to get his people to talk to our people before signing any contract!' But we had got him. It hardly ever works out like that, it was a clear shot with no branches or foliage in the way, the light was perfect, the digital sound was stunning, and we didn't have to climb seventy feet into the canopy to get it – some days just turn out right!

Sarah had to get back to London with the gilt-edged footage, while James and the rest of us spent the next ten days filming other activity in the rainforest, with some more singing apes. It seemed now that they all wanted to get in on the act, and just like London buses, turned up in threes and fours.

When the shoot was finished, James was meeting his wife for a holiday in southern Thailand. The others were moving elsewhere, and I was heading back to Blighty.

The only flight I could get on was a KLM 747 back to Amsterdam, and then on to Heathrow. I was bringing quite a few of the camera boxes back with me, and consequently had to pay a considerable amount of excess baggage on only one air ticket.

I had checked in at Bangkok airport the usual two and a half hours before the flight, due to the amount of film equipment I had, and all was fine except for having to pay the excess baggage. This would be no problem as I had 2,000 US dollars plus some sterling if needed.

Usually, you have to pay the excess before they load the film equipment on to the plane, but at Bangkok, or at least on that particular day, everything was loaded and I just had to pay.

A KLM steward took me to the appropriate office to pay the excess and left me with a charming young customs official. He was most interested in what I had been doing in the rainforest, as he had never been there. Whilst chatting, he was typing things into a computer, and making phone calls, some of them quite lengthy.

I noticed it was now only forty minutes to departure.

He finished a phone call, typed something into the computer, said, 'Excuse me,' and left.

When he hadn't returned after ten minutes, I became a little concerned, and went to look for help.

The charming young customs official returned and apologised for keeping me waiting, but didn't appear to be making any headway with the computer.

The terminal PA system informed everyone including me that it was fifteen minutes to the departure of the KLM flight to Amsterdam.

The young man made another phone call.

In a gesture intended to offer assistance, I indicated that the excess should be about $1,400 US.

The Director – the PA – and the Tick

He muttered 'Not straightforward.'
I said, 'Plane about to go.'
He said, 'Not long now.'

The PA announced, 'Would Mr Desmond please report for departure to Amsterdam as gate will close in two minutes.'

I said to young charming man 'That's me!'

He said, 'I know it,' and then added, 'KLM very good flight,' as if to assure me.

This time the PA was much more precise, 'This is the *final call* for Mr K Desmond for the KLM flight to Amsterdam – the gate is now closing.'

'I make phone call,' said the young man, who was becoming rapidly less charming, and more irritating.

'Police stop plane,' he announced.

'What?' I said.

'Police stop plane for you Mr Desmond – give me $1,700 US dollars.'

As I was counting out the dollars, two policemen arrived, and picked up my personal bags.

I thrust a bundle of dollars into the man's hand, which might have been around $1,700, and was told to hurry by the police.

As they hurried me away I heard the young man call, 'Have a nice life!' and then we were gone. The corridors I was being hurried along didn't appear to lead anywhere. Suddenly, we went through a door in a corridor that led directly on to the tarmac. There in front of me was the KLM 747 with the doors closed, but a motor-powered stairway was being driven to the plane.

I had kept the plane waiting almost fifteen minutes, which must have cost KLM quite a bit in turn-around time. This did not bode well for a twelve-hour flight to Amsterdam!

The stairway was now in place and the door had been opened. The two policemen indicated that I should follow them, and they hurried up the stairs with my bags.

We were met by two lovely female flight attendants, whose professional smiles were set in makeup the consistency of cement, and would never move again.

The plane was packed with very silent Dutch people, plus a few very silent Thai passengers, who all appeared to be looking in my direction, and must have wondered why the late arrival had been escorted to the plane by the police. Without doubt, an undesirable being removed from their country. Quite likely to be drugs. Could even be an ageing hippy!

The policemen had been bundled off the plane, and the cabin door virtually slammed behind them – I felt very alone.

A flight attendant, whose smile hadn't moved, led me down what felt like an endless aisle to my seat, which was fortunately on the end of a row.

As the 747 rolled along the taxiway, the Dutch captain, who obviously had unfortunate feelings about the English, made an apology to the passengers about the now 20-minute *delay* caused by the *late arrival* of *one* passenger who was *now seated* – Comfortably – *I hope*.'

I made a sort of apologetic gesture towards the man sitting next to me, which could have been taken to be friendly, but he didn't look up from his in-flight magazine. I decided to settle down and attempt to get some sleep to shorten the journey.

The 747 was at the end of the runway with the engines coming to speed, and that impressive surge of power when they reach full throttle and we started to roll. We must have just reached V2 and were committed to take off when two minute hot needles were inserted into the southern hemisphere of my left testicle, about where New Zealand would have been. The pain was vicious, and caused a hissing intake of breath.

The man with the in-flight magazine didn't flinch.

One might have expected the pain to ease a bit after a minute or so, but this wasn't the case.

I knew I had to investigate, but the seat belt sign was still illuminated.

It seemed like a day and a half before the sign was switched off. Then the last arrival on the plane, 'the drug smuggler – the ageing hippy' was the first on his feet shuffling down the aisle in hidden pain.

I reached the nearest toilets only to be confronted by a flight attendant whose make-up was the wrong mix for sustaining a permanent smile.

'Is there anything the matter?' she asked.

The Director – the PA – and the Tick

'No,' I lied, and shut the toilet door.

My trousers and underpants were round my ankles in record speed, and on close inspection there was a large black tick swinging on its incisors from the bottom of my left testicle. It was large because it was filled with my blood.

Now I knew that to remove it was necessary. I had been told the best way was neat alcohol applied directly and the tick would withdraw its incisors and fall off. Another method of removal was more drastic, and usually only suggested by women. One takes a lighted cigarette and applies it to the tick, trying to avoid igniting one's pubic hair. I had neither alcohol nor a cigarette, not that I would have experimented with the latter.

It was at that moment I think I lost my presence of mind. The tick was still there and appeared to be getting larger with more of my blood. I threw caution to the wind, and took hold of the tick in my fingernails and ripped it out. My eyes watered considerably, – this had not been a good idea.

Blood splattered down the side of the fixtures, down my legs, and some on my shoes.

Unfortunately, the tick's incisors were still embedded in New Zealand.

I thought, I am not going to dig them out, but I must clean them with something to reduce the chance of infection. I didn't think hot water would do the trick, but it was worth a try. The attempt was a bit painful.

A knock at the door, and the flight attendant asked, 'Is everything alright?'

'Yes,' I lied again.

'Let me know if you need anything,' she said.

'Do you serve gin and tonic in the toilets?' I asked.

'No, we do not.'

'You could hold the tonic, if you wished,' I said pathetically.

There was no reply.

Suddenly, I noticed that KLM, who think of everything, had a small bottle of cologne/aftershave by the tissues on a shelf above the basin. How I had missed this I didn't know, but I suppose I'd been too engrossed with goings on in New Zealand, as that was where the action had been.

My thinking was that this small bottle could contain some alcohol and possibly do the necessary. I took the cap off the bottle and splashed a good amount on to what now looked like a war zone. What happened in the next few minutes I am not quite certain. I know I banged the wall loudly, and said, '*Neeeaaarrrggghh!*' at least twice. I grabbed my shirt flap, which eventually ripped, and I bit my thumb, which drew more blood.

'Is everything alright in there?' enquired a male steward's voice. 'Do you require medical attention?'

'No!' I lied yet again.

I knew I had to get out of there, but I couldn't leave the place covered in blood. I washed the blood off the walls and the washbasin, pulled up my underpants and stuffed a dozen or so tissues inside them to absorb any blood.

I opened the door to find two attendants waiting for me.

'Alright?' said one.

'Alright,' I replied.

'Can you walk alright?' asked the other one, looking down and noticing the large deformity in my trousers orchestrated by the tissues.

'I'll manage okay.'

I realised I was walking much slower on the return journey to my seat, and dragging my left leg a little. Most of the passengers were looking away from me this time or looking down, apart from one elderly lady, who had spotted the blood on my shoes.

I noticed she had sent for the flight attendant, and they both looked in my direction, but only for a moment, as they noticed I was looking back at them. The attendant went back to the galley for a few minutes, and then walked down the aisle to me.

'It looks as though you may have some blood on your shoes,' she said.

'I believe I have,' I replied.

'Well, I thought you should know,' she said.

'I do.'

'Well then,' she half smiled, 'that's alright then.'

'I imagine it is,' I said, and smiled.

The remainder of the journey home was uneventful.

Eric Hebborn – Master Forger

I met Eric Hebborn at his home in the hills a few miles east of Rome. I was part of a small crew who had been commissioned to make a TV documentary on one of the most talented artists of the last century. The difference with this artist was that at the time of the filming, very few people had heard of him. He, however, had just finished his autobiography and our film was to coincide with its launch. This would introduce him to thousands around the world who had a passion for art.

A handful of art dealers in London and Rome knew him well. They had been pleased to know him over the previous twenty years, as their establishments had enjoyed a modest amount of success due to Eric's skills.

For some years Eric had produced remarkable ink and wash drawings in the style of sixteenth, seventeenth and eighteenth century masters. Piranesi, Parmigianino and Pontormo were some of the painters whose 'preparatory drawings' sold through the auction rooms in Rome and London.

It must be made clear from the outset that Eric Hebborn never told anyone these drawings were by any particular artist; he simply stated they had been found. Art dealers and connoisseurs in Europe and America were pleased to give the works their own provenance, and with lire, sterling and dollars looming large on the horizon, also indicated their probable value at auction.

In the interview, Eric Hebborn was compelling and entertaining. He told our director, Benham Gooder, that he was born in London in 1934 and his dad was a grocer's assistant. The family moved from South London to Romford in Essex just close to Gallows Corner, and a few years later on to Harold Wood.

While at school in Harold Wood, Eric had deliberately set fire to a cloakroom, to offset the injustice of being caned for possessing a match and a piece of sandpaper he was using in art class.

The school apparently didn't share his logic about torching the school to offset the punishment already received, and he was sent to the local borstal.

Eventually, his academic career took him to Wandsworth College of Art and the Royal Academy, where he was awarded the Silver Medal, which led to a scholarship in Rome. It became rapidly clear to those who knew him, as an artist and draughtsman, Eric was in the Premier League.

His skills became more apparent when he joined a restoration company in Haunch of Venison Yard. This location was minutes from Sotheby's and many other prominent art dealers in Bond Street. Eric told us that this proved to be the best move he had ever made, as Mr Aczel, the owner, passed on to Eric the finer skills and secrets of picture restoration. He went on to say that he always had difficulty in judging where the fine line was between 'restoration' and 'repainting'.

One of his major discoveries with Mr Aczel was – 'art is business'. A painting of Joseph, Mary and the baby Jesus, would sell for much more at auction if it was a 'Madonna and Child' with Joseph having been painted out. Eric realised dealers are businessmen, and always prefer a picture that will sell.

I remember him saying to me later on, 'You're a Yorkshireman, you'll understand this. Pictures that are difficult to sell are bad business, and by some strange quirk of logic become bad art.'

During his time with Mr Aczel, Eric was offered quite a few pictures from respected dealers that required some 'improvement'!

As Eric wrote in his autobiography *Drawn to Trouble* – how the old masters that left Mr Aczel looking as good as new (if not better) would soon be presented in the galleries of the well-respected dealers for whom they had been doctored.

Enriched by his experiences and knowledge gained in Haunch of Venison Yard, plus his scholarship from Rome, Eric decided it was time for him to branch out on his own, and see how many 'old masters' he could find.

A friend of his, Sir Anthony Blunt, who at the time was Surveyor the Queen's Pictures, was shown some of Eric's ink and wash drawings, and asked for his opinion. Sir Anthony was complimentary and showed some appreciation of the drawings, but did feel Eric's draughtsmanship was lacking. One could argue that the very position Blunt held in the world of art did give him the necessary eye to spot inferior draughtsmanship. Eric, on the other hand, did not quite see things that way and was still smarting considerably from the remarks.

Some time late in the 1960s, very gradually, drawings from the eighteenth century French School appeared in London and in Rome. Most of these were finished in black and red chalks. At the same time a clutch of Stefano Della Bella (1610-1664) preparatory studies appeared for sale at London auctions. Colnaghi's sold one of the French School drawings at their summer exhibition of 1969 and Sotheby's exhibited and sold another in December of 1969. Both galleries had given the drawings the provenance on which they were sold. Colnaghi's also bought some of the Stefano Della Bella studies, and Eric Hebborn – 'art dealer' – went back to Rome richer than when he arrived.

'But where did you get hold of sixteenth and seventeenth century paper?' asked Benham.

'Italy, particularly Rome and Florence. Both cities have many old bookshops and markets, which had a quantity of books from that period that they were unable to sell, possibly because of damage or simply age. I went to these places, and to the delight of the proprietor I bought many of his un-sellable old books. Most of the books are in a terrible condition but they all had a flyleaf in the front and back, which had been protected by the hard cover. Some of the books from the sixteenth century had a flyleaf made from vellum. All I did was to remove the paper or vellum, discard the remains of the book, and I had an instant collection of material to work on. If the owners of the bookshops thought I was a little crazy, well, so be it.'

'How did you become involved with Hans Calmann?' asked our director.

Hans Calmann was a dealer who specialised in drawings of the seventeenth and eighteenth centuries and had handled a quantity of old masters only equalled by Colnaghi's. Eric knew that Calmann often visited Rome to search out any new finds on the drawings market. On these trips to Rome Calmann would invariably visit Edoardo, an art dealer who happened to be an old friend of Eric's and had sold some of Eric's drawings. With the information that Calmann was due to visit Rome, Eric told us he set a trap for him.

Eric put some of his drawings in a folder for Edoardo to show Calmann. Included in the folder was a photograph of another of Eric's drawings 'after the style of Mantegna'. This particular drawing had been purchased by Colnaghi's from Eric when last in London. Calmann had seen the drawing at Colnaghi's and expressed considerable interest. On the back of the photo in the folder, Eric had written the name and address of his studio on the outskirts of Rome.

Calmann was delighted when Edoardo showed him the folder containing a batch of newly discovered drawings, and of course recognised the drawing in the photo, as the one he had previously seen at Colnaghi's in Old Bond Street. The address on the back of the photo was all that he needed. The trap was sprung.

The following day Calmann hurried, as quickly as his large frame would allow, up the steep hill to the address on the photo, where Eric was waiting for him.

After brief introductions, Eric said, 'Calmann showed me the drawings purchased from Edoardo the previous day, expressing surprise at finding drawings of such fine quality and superb draughtsmanship, and could my sources possibly acquire any more?'

Eric told Calmann he would certainly keep his eye open for them.

Then to Eric's total amusement, while Calmann was showing him the drawings he had bought from Edoardo, he explained to Eric what to look out for, the usual telltale signs of the forger, in case Eric was duped by some sharp dealer.

Eric assured him he would be on his guard.

Calmann asked Eric to show him any other drawings he might have at his gallery; after all, there might just be something which would interest him.

They both went through a pile of drawings of varying styles, Calmann showing an ever-increasing degree of pleasure the more he handled.

Eric told us the funniest moment came when Calmann pointed out the excellent pen and wash skill some of them showed, and then identified most of them, quite naturally believing Eric had never seen them before.

Apparently, Calmann's discovery of a new gallery in Rome had brought him such satisfaction that he purchased a few more drawings.

Eric told us he thought we would like to know that one of those drawings was reproduced in *The Burlington Magazine* in November 1969. The drawing had been attributed to a Jan Spaekert and called '*Biblical Scene*'. Eric went on to tell us that he had never heard of Jan Spaekert before or since, and when he had made the drawing he simply did it in the style of a northern Italian school vaguely linked with the work of Michelangelo.

As Eric said, 'This was a perfect example of a dealer desperately attempting to put a name and provenance to an unknown work at all costs.'

Over the next ten years, Hans Calmann along with Sotheby's, Christie's and Colnaghi, plus Christie's in Rome, bought well over a hundred drawings from Eric; some have estimated the number to be far greater.

Eric argued that should the forger require a yardstick to measure success. When you have seen one of your drawings advertised in *The Burlington Magazine* by Colnaghi, as a 'Van Dyke' *Christ Crowned with Thorns* pen and ink with brown wash, then to learn that Colnaghi's had sold it to the British Museum – you could consider that as some kind of success.

Perhaps on the other hand, the pen and bistre preparatory study Hans Calmann purchased and sold to the National Gallery of Denmark, attributing it to 'Giovanni Battista Piranesi' *Preparatory Study for an Etching* could be classed as modestly successful.

Benham then asked Eric, 'Why have you chosen this particular time to blow your cover?'

'I'm tired of the subterfuge, and I want to spend time painting my own stuff, particularly watercolours. Also there are a few people in London who have smelt a rat, and I believe I am the one carrying that smell. After all I have shown the art market to be corrupt, insomuch that a dealer will give an attribution to almost any half-decent drawing, and you must believe me, some of my early drawings were only half decent,' he said with a smile.

'Have any of the museums discovered they have a "fake" hanging on their wall?'

'The curator of the Pierpont Morgan Library suddenly tumbled that the Francesco del Cossa *Pageboy with a Lance* could possibly be a fake. A colleague of hers in the National Gallery of Washington had noticed that two Cossas owned by the gallery looked remarkably similar, the wash finish being very like the other. She could do well to have a closer look at the Pageboy she possessed.'

'Apparently, the story goes that she approached the Cossa with a "doubting eye" and suddenly it was obvious to her that it was "suspect". I can only wonder why she didn't bring her "doubting eye" along when purchasing the drawing for the library ten years previously. It had taken her a long time to suddenly suspect!'

Eric continued, 'Colnaghi's were informed of the situation, and carried out thorough scientific tests which failed to prove that any of the drawings were forgeries, but Colnaghi's did return the original purchase price to their client.'

The interview with Eric was a huge success, and our director was well pleased. I was sorry to leave Eric, we had filmed him drawing and painting in the style of the fifteenth and sixteenth century and his immense skill and draughtsmanship was apparent to each of us. He was without doubt a man of charm and immense talent.

On our return to London we were not too surprised to find that only one dealer was prepared to talk to us. Julian Stock was a Director at Sotheby's and gave us a very frank and informative interview. He explained to us that Eric Hebborn was the very finest of draughtsman, and quite likely the greatest faker ever. I wondered whether Sir Anthony Blunt still doubted Eric's draughtsmanship.

When Christie's were phoned, Benham received a courteous, 'No comment.'

Eric's autobiography *Drawn to Trouble* was published on November 4th 1991, and BBC *Omnibus* transmitted our documentary on November 8th. There was the anticipated buzz in the art world, and one or two 'connoisseurs' declared, with the twenty-twenty vision of hindsight, that they had suspected Hebborn for quite some time. If this was true, why hadn't any of them or any of the dealers brought any legal action against Eric Hebborn?

As was said at the time in the *Evening Standard*, 'Eric Hebborn's 'best protection seems to have been the homosexual art mafia, which helped him move onwards and upwards, and deflected the curious.'

Eric was murdered one cold night in January 1996 in a back street in Rome. He was 61-years-old. The investigation stated that heavy blows had crushed his skull. So far there has been no conviction.

The Final Chapter

Over the past thirty-eight years, I have occasionally been asked to record talks, speeches, debates, lectures etc. These are usually for archive purposes or reference, not for broadcast.

It's always refreshing to work on your own and not to be hampered by production, or directors, as they always want to get involved, and usually know very little about sound. The exception, of course, is Nick Broomfield.

The speakers requiring these recordings are legion, and some have requested to be 'off the record' which always seems to me, a contradiction in terms. They do, however, cover a wide range, from party political to weddings, military campaigns to sermons, investment deals in the arms trade to school speech days.

University lecturers are, in the main, interesting if sometimes a little eccentric, but I usually come away with a bit of a buzz.

In 1972 the inventor of the bouncing bomb, Barnes Wallis, gave a brilliant talk on the future of car design, and within fifteen years he was proved to be absolutely correct; but then a car ought to be a piece of cake if you have invented a bomb with the ability to bounce, and survived the experience.

Scientists, and psychologists can be of good value, but often lean towards the equation, mathematical theory and *how* things come together, rather than *why*. History professors are interesting, and often quite stimulating.

In October 2001 I was completely gripped by a recording of Dr John Blanchard, a Christian apologist who had given his talk the title 'Does God Believe in Atheists?' Now for me, I'm hooked by the title, and when he started with:

> *Bertrand Russell was one of the most colourful thinkers of the 20th century, a Nobel Prize winner, an author of over sixty books on such diverse subjects as logic, China, Communism, mathematics and religion. A passionate and dogmatic atheist, Russell believed that 'the world is simply there, and has no explanation' and that man was the outcome of 'accidental collocations of atoms'.*

The Final Chapter

> *When asked by a colleague, 'What will you say if you ever meet God, and he asks you why did you not believe in Him?' Russell replied, 'I shall look him straight in the eye and say – Not enough evidence.'*
>
> *If Russell was wrong, he could not have made a more terrible or tragic mistake, and I want to look at four of the most powerful pieces of evidence to suggest he was wrong.'*

By now Dr Blanchard had me totally hooked, and most of the remainder of the chapter are in his words.

> *The first piece of evidence is the existence and nature of the universe. Stephen Hawking, possibly the best-known scientist in the world today, has a fascinating description of Earth – 'a medium sized planet orbiting around an average star in the outer suburbs of an ordinary spiral galaxy'. This is true, but it hides the vastness involved in, let's say, the Milky Way, that measures 621 thousand million million miles across and contains 100 thousand million stars and is one of 100 thousand million galaxies known to us.*
>
> *This 'medium sized planet,' our Earth, is 8,000 miles in diameter, 25,000 miles in circumference, and has a surface area of 200 million square miles. The 'average star' is what we call the Sun, which is a million times the size of the Earth.*

Whilst on our shoot for Survival TV with Richard Leakey in 1974, our camp was on the eastern side of Lake Rudolf (now Lake Turkana). In our first week, both David and I noticed a huge white cloud in the night sky. The surprising feature about this particular white cloud was that every night it turned up in the same place, was the same shape and never moved. Another remarkable feature was the brightness of the cloud. In fact, it was so bright it was just about possible to read a book by the light it gave out. About the third night, as we sat by the lake counting crocodile eyes, we pointed out the incredible cloud to someone, just in case they hadn't spotted the phenomenon, when they in turn revealed to us that it wasn't a cloud, but the Milky Way. We all made noises indicating that we knew that already, and we thought it just had the 'appearance' of a cloud. The newcomer was polite enough not to point out the error in our logic, and simply told us that when you put a few hundred million stars together and spread them across the night sky, it certainly can take on the 'appearance' of a large, bright cloud.

Now this has to beg the question – How did these galaxies get there?

Dr Blanchard explained that the most widely accepted theory today was that of the 'Big Bang'.

> *The Big Bang model says that some 15 billion years ago our universe was so minute it could be passed through the eye of a needle. Many scientists then tell us that a massive explosion, followed by 15 billion years of expansion produced the universe as we now have it.*
>
> *This raises obvious questions – Where did the speck of dust come from? Why was the speck of dust there? Why wasn't it somewhere else? Was there anywhere else for it to be that it could have been? These are all questions the atheist has difficulty in answering.*

He then went on to point out that the Big Bang could not in the strictest sense be called a theory. For anything to qualify as an accepted theory, the components involved must be tested hundreds, and sometimes thousands of times, and when all the tests are completed and give a common result, the outcome can be said to be a cogent, tested, credible scientific theory. The Big Bang, as its name suggests, cannot be tested at all, let alone a hundred times. If true, it was a one-off, and as such is only an idea, a model, and it is one that many leading scientists question or reject.

> *Some scientists accept the Big Bang idea, and others reject it. Roger Penrose, a scientist and mathematician who has worked with Stephen Hawking on the existence of black holes was asked if the Big Bang could be a mathematical possibility. According to Roger Penrose the odds against the Big Bang resulting in the ordered universe of which we are part would be 1 in 10 raised to the power of 10 raised to the power of 123. This number is so absurdly large*

that it is said to have more zeros than the total number of particles in the entire universe!

What is more, all the evidence we have shows clearly that explosions produce disorder, not order. Tragically, we had evidence of this on September 11th 2001 in the destruction of the twin towers of the World Trade Centre in New York. If you had been in New York on that afternoon you would have found, not order, elegance or design, but 1.5 million tons of rubble and a grave for nearly three thousand people. Explosions cause chaos and disorder.

There are only three possibilities as to the origin of the universe: One is that it is eternal (which seems to be what Bertrand Russell meant by saying 'It's just there'). A second is that it self-created. The third is that it was created by an eternal self-existent Power.

The Bertrand Russell theory that the universe is eternal is often known as the 'steady state theory', and was shared by people like Fred Hoyle and others some fifty years ago. Since then, science has shown that matter is constantly changing, and has no certain stability, and the 'steady state theory' has now been almost universally abandoned.

The second idea, that the universe self-created, became all the rage in the early part of the last century. Now you don't have to be too much of a genius to spot the weakness in the plot. If something is self-created, then the something had to exist before it existed in order to bring itself into existence, because if it didn't exist before, it would be unable to bring itself into existence.

'The third, and only other possibility, is that the universe was created by an eternal self-existent Power, and the Omnipotent, Everlasting God of the Bible fits the bill. At the beginning of the Bible we can read: 'In the beginning God created the heavens and the earth' and towards the end of the Bible we read: 'By faith we understand that the universe was formed at God's command.'

Everything that had a beginning had a cause. The universe had a beginning and therefore had a cause. The God revealed in the Bible is a credible cause.

The universe also has an ordered nature, governed by the universal and dependable laws of physics. This is why we can fly men to the moon, – and boil eggs. These certainties, these dependable laws of physics, provide massive problems for the atheist. The model chosen by the atheist has existence without a creator, order without intelligence, laws without a legislator, and design without a designer.

The second major problem for the atheist is the mystery of life. The Encyclopaedia Britannica tells us that 'there is no generally accepted definition of life.' This is remarkable! We know that a donkey has life, but a diamond doesn't, that a tree has life, but a concrete post doesn't – yet apparently we can't define what it is.

In 1953 Francis Crick and his colleague James Watson announced to the world that they had found 'the secret of life'. What they actually meant was that they had discovered the double helical structure of DNA, which governs all biological reproduction. DNA is what triggers into action all the bits and pieces that a living organism needs in order for it to become a living organism. Without DNA the amino acids and all the other interesting biological bric-a-brac would just be lying around like pieces of Lego – getting nowhere.'

Where did DNA come from? What kick started DNA?

The bottom line is that DNA houses genetic information – lots of it!

The information in a single chromosome contains the equivalent of 500 million words. That is 2,000 books of 650 pages each.

A single fertilised human egg – contains 23 pairs of chromosomes – that is 46 chromosomes, which means that the genetic information in one fertilised human egg is the equivalent of 90,000 books of 650 pages per book. Now if the information in DNA is not the product of DNA where did it come from?

The atheist says 'It just happened.' George Wald, a Harvard scientist, and joint winner in 1967 of the Nobel Prize for Physiology, said 'When it comes to the origin of life on earth there are only two possibilities – creation or spontaneous generation.

Spontaneous generation was disproved one hundred years ago, but that leads us to only one other conclusion, that of supernatural creation. We cannot accept that, therefore we choose to believe the impossible, that life arose spontaneously by chance.'

The Law of Biogenesis says 'that life comes only from life' – and the eternal, self-existent, life-giving God of the Bible provides the necessary origin.

Richard Dawkins, Professor of the Public Understanding of Science at Oxford University, says pretty much the same thing as George Wald. Dawkins says that life began with a self-replicating molecule which he calls 'The Replicator.' We know there are self-replicating molecules in the world today, but Dawkins says that the very first one came about 'by accident.' But he invents the 'accident' because he can't tolerate the alternative. As he himself puts it, 'The obvious alternative to chance is an intelligent designer – but I'm afraid I shall give God very short shrift.' Dawkins believes that we live in a universe in which there is "No design, no purpose, no evil and no good, nothing but blind pitiless indifference." If Dawkins is right, then the loss of life in the Twin Towers in New York was a meaningless event in a meaningless world, and there is no reason for Dawkins or any of us to feel grief, pain, loss or anger. But atheists around the world did feel all these emotions – why?

I heard recently that the genetic code of one single bacterium is far more complex than Windows 98. Now can anybody believe that Windows 98 came about by 'accident'? I find it difficult to believe that Bill Gates accidentally tripped down the stairs one day and that the result was Windows 98. Without God there is no other credible reason for the existence of life.

Atheism's third problem is the marvel of mankind. Prof. CEM Joad famously said that a human body had enough fat to make seven bars of soap, enough iron to make one medium sized nail, enough sugar to sweeten seven cups of tea, enough lime to whitewash one chicken coup, enough phosphorous to tip 2000 matches, enough magnesium to provide one dose of salts, enough potash to explode one toy cannon, and enough sulphur to rid one average size dog of fleas.

The Final Chapter

Well now you know what you are – more or less.

A human body is a truly wondrous thing. Think of the human frame with its 100 joints, 200 bones, and 600 muscles all working perfectly together. The tendons, which anchor the muscles to the bone, could withstand pressure of eight tons per square inch. The human hand is a phenomenal instrument with 652,000 nerve endings in it, strong enough to wield an axe, yet delicate enough to conduct microsurgery. The eye is an amazing phenomenon. It processes 80% of the information that comes to us, and can deal with 500,000 messages simultaneously. The retina – just one square inch – contains 130 million receptor cells and they are not all identical – 124 million are rod shaped, and distinguish between light and darkness, the remaining six million are cone shaped and can distinguish between eight million variations of colour. The human heart beats about 40 million times a year, pumping blood through an accumulation of 80,000 miles of blood vessels. One drop of human blood contains 250 million cells of three different kinds in exactly the right proportions. The brain accounts for only 2% of an average persons body weight, but it is an amazing amalgamation of material. It has 100 billion neurones – what people like you and me would call nerve cells – and each one of these nerve cells has up to 100 thousand connections with other parts of the brain.

Some people say the brain is rather like a computer – a sort of super-computer – but there is no comparison between a brain and a computer. Think of the capability of a brain compared to that of a computer. Computers can't express love, hatred, joy, pride, frustration, anger – we can.

Computers can't enjoy music or a wonderful sunset. Computers don't know that they are computers. Computers can't invent brains – brains can invent computers.

To say that computers are rather like brains is like saying that elephants are rather like oranges.

The human body is truly amazing – and the whole package comes shrink wrapped in three layers of waterproof covering with its own built-in air conditioning system. Are we really to believe all that came about by 'accident?'

I suggest it is infinitely easier, and requires less faith, to agree with the psalmist when he says to God (Psalm 139) 'You created my inmost being, you knit me together in my mothers womb. I praise you because I am fearfully and wonderfully made.'

Think about this. It takes less faith to believe this, than to declare 'I am a fearful and wonderful accident.' – That takes a massive amount of faith!'

Then think of man's moral dimension. Do all living creatures have intrinsic moral values? Do they have codes of moral conduct? Can animals have similar rights to humans if those rights are not balanced by responsibilities? Are animals answerable for their actions? Should cats who play with wounded mice be brought to account? Do ants, sheep and kangaroos wrestle with moral issues? If we should give 'rights' to whales, dolphins and gorillas, why not to hyenas, jellyfish and dung-beetles?

The logic seems unanswerable. The plain fact is that there is a massive chasm separating humankind from everything else we see or know. Those who argue that as apes are almost genetically identical to humans they should be accorded the equivalent of human rights are missing a crucial point made in New Scientist: 'Genomes are not recipes. A creature that shares 98.4% of DNA with humans is not 98.4% human, any more than a fish that shares, say, 40% is 40% human.'

Human beings have a sense of right and wrong. We can speak about justice and fairness, and of things being good and bad – where did we get those ideas? How can we jump from the so called 'Big Bang' 15 billion years ago to the mysterious origin of some form of life – which we can't define – and then to morality which understands fairness and justice, right and wrong? How can we jump from atoms to ethics and from molecules to morality?

Human beings have consciences, and the conscience reacts when a law is broken. Why is there a law? – And why should we have consciences? Why are we in tune with a moral law, which we never brought into being?

Not everybody has identical moral standards, but there is an amazing consensus about basic values even when there is no written human code involved. I have never come across a written human code against greed, selfishness, covetousness, envy, jealousy, or pride. As far as I know it there is no human law against any of those things anywhere in the world. Then why do all of us think it is right to call these things wrong?

What is more, human beings have a spiritual dimension. Man is a religious animal – he must, and will, have some religion. The British scientist Sir John Houghton stated, 'There is general evidence that most human beings from whatever part of the world, and from the earliest times have exhibited a fundamental belief in a Divine Being or beings.' Why? Why are we apparently the only species which does that? Wolves don't worship. Snakes don't hold services. Not even the praying mantis prays. Yet in every culture we have been able to uncover, there is evidence that humans have what the mathematical genius Blaise Pascal called 'a God shaped vacuum.' Why?

Richard Dawkins has an explanation. He says 'it is a virus of the brain' – and goes on to say that teaching your children from the Bible should be prosecuted as mental child abuse.

Dawkins practices his militant atheism within yards of where people of outstanding moral integrity and fibre were burned at the stake rather than deny the God of the Bible as a dynamic living reality who deserves to be worshipped in the manner he has ordained.

Is Richard Dawkins qualified to brush their testimonies aside as a 'virus'?

Millions of people over thousands of years have demonstrated that this is not the case. Man has a spiritual need – and only the God revealed in Scripture can meet it.

Finally, atheism has the problem of one particular human life. Sir Isaac Newton, the father of modern science, called the Bible ' a rock from which all the hammers of criticism have never chipped a single fragment'. It is an infallible database that can be trusted implicitly, including what it tells us about one particular person – Jesus of Nazareth.

The Final Chapter

Hundreds of years before Jesus was born, God promised through precise prophecy that he would intervene in human history by sending the deliverer – the Messiah – who would provide the perfect answer to man's greatest need. The prophecies numbered over 300, covering the timing and exact place of his birth, his family tree, his lifestyle, his teaching, his miraculous powers and minute details of the events surrounding his death. The prophets even told that he would be born of a virgin.

Jesus fulfilled every one of these prophecies to the letter. But why did he come? The Bible could not be clearer. He did not come as a politician, a diplomat, an economist, a scientist, a doctor or a psychiatrist.

He did come to deal with our most radical, universal and deadly problem – it is what the Bible uncompromisingly calls 'sin'.

Some time ago an article in *The Times* newspaper asked the question, 'What's wrong with the world?'

In the replies to the newspaper that followed, the shortest letter was by far the best:

> In response to your question, 'What's wrong with the world?' – I am.
>
> Yours faithfully,
>
> G K Chesterton.

The media today is clogged with reports of violence, bloodshed, racism, murder, debauchery, wars, immorality, deceit, corruption, greed and sin of every kind.

A terrorist attack that slaughters 3,000 people between sunrise and noon is shocking, but should not surprise us. The root cause of such horrendous happening is not to be found in American foreign policy, Middle East politics or religious fanaticism, but in the depravity of the human heart, which is 'deceitful above all things and beyond cure.' (Jeremiah 17:9).

It is this horrific problem that God came to solve in the person of His Son Jesus – who in doing so he endured to the full the suffering and pain that sin causes. He endured devastating agony and pain as he hung on a cross in our place, and for the first time in his human existence, lost sight of his father's face, as your sin, and my sin, and the sin of the world caused his heart to explode – and with an eternal cry, 'It is finished,' he died for us all.

> *Jesus was unique in his conception, wisdom, miracles, character, death and resurrection. If he told the truth, we may know that God is a Living, Sovereign Reality.*
>
> *The existence or non-existence of God does not depend on how many experts can be quoted, but on the person and work of Jesus of Nazareth.*

Reflect for a moment on these words written in the 1960s:

> At the end of time, billions of people were standing about on a great plain before God's throne. Most shrank from the brilliant light that was before them. But some groups near the front talked heatedly – not with cringing shame but with belligerence.
>
> 'Can God judge us?'
>
> 'What right has he got to pass judgement?'
>
> 'How can he know about suffering?' said a young brunette. She ripped open her sleeve to reveal a tattooed number on her arm from a Nazi concentration camp. 'We endured terror... beating... torture... death!'
>
> In another group a black man lowered his collar. 'What about this?' he said, showing an ugly rope burn. 'I was lynched for no crime but being black!'
>
> In another crowd, a pregnant schoolgirl muttered, 'Why should I suffer?' 'It wasn't my fault.'
>
> Stretching across the plain there were hundreds of such groups. Each had a complaint against God for the evil and suffering he had permitted in his world. How lucky God was to live in heaven where all was sweetness and light, where there was no weeping or fear, no hunger or hatred!
>
> What did God know of all that men had been forced to

The Final Chapter

endure in this world? 'For God leads a pretty sheltered life,' they said.

So each of these groups sent forward their leader, chosen from those who had suffered the most.

A Jew, a black man, a victim from Hiroshima, a horribly disabled arthritic, a thalidomide child, a teenager who had lost limbs from meningitis, and many others.

In the centre of the plain they all consulted with each other.

Eventually they were ready to present their case. It was rather clever. Before God could be qualified to be their Judge, he must endure what they had endured. Their verdict was that God should be sentenced to live on earth – as a man! Let him be born a Jew. Let the legitimacy of his birth be doubted. Give him a job so difficult that even his family will think him out of his mind when he tries to do it. Let him be betrayed by his closest friends. Let him face false charges, be tried by a prejudiced jury and convicted by a cowardly judge. Let him be tortured. Then at last, let him see what it means to be terribly alone. Then let him die in agony. Let him die so there can be no doubt that he has died. Let there be a whole host of witnesses to verify it.

As each leader announced the portion of his sentence, a loud murmur of approval went up from the people assembled.

When the last had finished pronouncing sentence there was a long silence.

No one uttered a word.

No one moved.

Suddenly, all knew that God had already served his sentence.

The choice we each make, is whether to travel the path with the atheist, the cynic, and sceptic, along with Richard Dawkins, and follow Bertrand Russell into his 'nothing'. Without a change of heart, the hideous tragedy for Russell on 2nd February 1970 when he stepped from death into eternity was to discover 'overwhelming evidence for God', and not a 'lack of evidence' as he had professed. When he attempted to look God in the eye, Russell's vast knowledge and understanding appeared as a transient vapour set against the splendour, and dazzling brilliance of light surrounding him (ref. Revelation 22:3-5). He then knew this was God, this His Glory, this His Light, that he was about to be separated from, for all eternity. As someone has rightly said, 'There are no atheists in Hell.'

Or, we can choose the alternative. Total forgiveness offered through the love of God by His Son Jesus, His death, His Resurrection, enabling us to spend all eternity in His glorious presence, forever. Only by God's grace can we enter, but we must first recognise our desperate need for God's everlasting love, and turn to Him in faith.

On the 3rd August 1650, Oliver Cromwell made an impassioned plea to the General Assembly in Scotland, and those same words echo down the centuries to us now.

I beseech you, in the bowels of Christ, think it possible you may be mistaken.

Sounds Personal

An appreciation of all those who have offered encouragement, friendship, and work, which shaped and influenced my life over the past forty years.

Amir Amirani

Your film on the Blue Plaque for Jimi Hendrix was a winner, as was your film on Awards, but my heart was stolen by the *Waterworks* – Richard was a pleasure to work with, and totally incorrigible. I shall never forget his touching gesture at the graveside of Peter Pears and Benjamin Britten. Where do you find remarkable people like him?

Taghi Amirani

Not many have turned documentary film around as you did, and each time it not only worked well, but was exciting to observe and be part of.

Earth Calling Basingstoke – wonderful and inventive – was like working in a refreshing breeze for the first time. Each day you produced a new method of realising the craft I had worked in for almost thirty years. It was like having the scales removed from my eyes and the clouds surrounding my imagination blown away.

Vegetable Plots – one of the best documentaries I have worked on. Thank you for putting me in touch with such warm and generous people, particularly Charlie.

Holy Places – a remarkable journey through a spiritual plain. Your understanding of these people and their deeply held faiths reflected an integrity seldom found in our industry.

The introduction to Googoosh at Wembley and to hear her sing was thrilling, and more recently, the music of Afghanistan at the Royal Albert Hall – thanks for making these things possible.

I only mention a few of the many films you have made, each one a discovery in its own right, and by now I expect you have discovered the answer to your question, 'What are we doing here?'

Martin Bell

I had never worked with a 'listening' cameraman before – you people are rare, and when discovered, like gold dust. It was good to watch you shoot on the early documentaries, particularly *In Loving Memories* – I learnt a lot about 'living camerawork'. Thanks for your patience – the wonderful shoots in Africa and the UK, but I guess the streets of Seattle is where we were both changed. I thank you for keeping me safe on those streets, and together with Mary-Ellen, steering us through a truly remarkable film.

Working with you in southern Iraq on *Tigris* with the Marsh Arabs and Thor Heyerdahl will always be a special part of my life.

I'm not sure I ever thanked you fully for scraping me off the Narok Road in Kenya and getting me to the nearest hospital. The medics who have since examined me remarked that this was probably a major factor contributing to my beating a coma over the line.

I can only apologise for not recognising you in Nairobi Hospital a week later when you leant over the bed to wish me well – can't think what came over me.

Thanks for being there, Martin.

Dr John Blanchard

The final chapter would not be there without your guidance, encouragement and 'tweaking'. Thank you for agreeing to my use of your lecture of October 2001, which stated clearly all I wished to but was unable to say.

Patrick Boland

You are a most encouraging student. I applaud you for the work you have accomplished and the awards you have received. I do thank you for your generosity in sharing with me an accolade most deservedly yours.

Emma Bowman

Your skill, tenacity and diplomacy enabled us to interview people in situations we could never have managed without you. Some of the stunning content Chris and I shot was down to your dogged determination.

How you steered us around the police in Manchester I'll never know – but you were good. It's hardly surprising Chris affectionately calls you 'bulldog'.

Thanks for providing a good atmosphere for us to work in, but particularly for the shirt. My family approved, but were concerned I was suddenly developing a 'lifestyle'.

Carrie Britton

Lady Guns – *Snappers* – *Whistleblowers* – what a special clutch of films to have taken part in! Hugh and Phil – both good people. The courage and undeniable integrity of the contributors to *Whistleblowers*! I must thank you for turning me into a 'gentleman' – complete with green wellies – inside twenty minutes. Never forgetting the introduction I had to the lovely Ash Priors, the mysterious Langley Marsh, the dashing Preston Bowyer or the incredibly wicked Lydeard St Lawrence. Is he still 'serving time'?

Brian Clarke

I must record my thanks for your friendship, concern and thoughtfulness in 1980 when I turned up on crutches, and you offered me some gentle work at the light box in Audio Engineering. This was a difficult time, and climbing three flights of stairs every day proved to be excellent therapy for me – the doctors at Barts Hospital were well pleased.

Michael Colomb

We certainly covered some unusual jobs in the early days of Better Sound, but I do thank you for pointing me in the right direction.

Andrea Cornes & Mark James

It's difficult to separate you two as most of the work I did for one, I did for the other. The films you involved me in always provided plenty of interest and pleasure. I knew we could be on to something totally different when *Upholding the Bricks*, a film about the artist Karl Andre, was planned in the USA and the UK. I do admit I was puzzled to hear that, although Karl Andre lived in America and we were in America, he wouldn't be turning up for the film all about him. This didn't appear to faze either of you, and your optimism shone through. You were right – it was a good film.

Red & Sexy – Through the Night – Trainsition – Freeze Frame – About Face and the many other films opened up elements of the art world very new to me. Damien Hurst is a bit 'different' for a lad from Leeds, but thank you all the same. Venice was sensational and I loved the experience.

Sarah Cunliffe

Whether as director, producer, doctor or friend, you are an exceptional lady. I'll never forget your care and determination to get me mobile in Thailand, or those sublime singing apes at Khao Yai, and how could I ever forget the journey home?

The orphaned orang-utans at Sepilok still haunt me from time to time, as do the beautiful sounds of that rainforest. The discovery of Booker T is still evident when being addressed by Chris Openshaw.

Sumatra, Way Kanan and those remarkable elephants! The unforgettable calls of the Siamangs – when I hear them today, its still a little unnerving. I shall always thank you for taking me to some of the most thrilling and beautiful places on the planet, and for the lasting memories.

Bruce Davidson

Big Bad Mzungu of Epulu – were there ever enough wrist watches to keep you out of jail? I hope your life with the gorillas continues to be enthralling and safe. Thank you for always being there when needed, and always doing the rotten jobs so willingly. I could never climb a tree like you, anyway.

John Dollar

I suppose waking up in a Bedouin tent at 4:30 a.m. and being told, 'The sun is rising in the wrong place,' will always remain a unique memory. I was even more amazed when you rapidly corrected the situation, and I doubt the camels even noticed.

Whether marvelling at the light and stillness in the Wadi Rumman, or heaving and rolling on the Irish Sea with a lone shark hunter poised for the kill, you certainly have the knack of placing a chap in the centre of adventure. A thirty-foot basking shark passing two feet away from our dinghy is always a thrilling memory! The shark can quite easily become 40-feet long, depending on the quality of the wine. Do you still have the blue beret last seen disappearing round a headland on Aisla Craig? Thank you for many hours of your peaceful company and the introductions to remarkable people. Never forgetting the day we spent at 'a rose-red city half as old as time'.

Only one thing I feel I ought to mention – don't try spiriting books out of the British Library – it doesn't work.

Neville & Beryl Druce

Neville Druce was without debate the finest teacher I have ever had. He not only taught me about sound and recording, but also the characteristics of microphones and introduced me to the world of acoustics. I would never have been able to record in certain situations and provide the impossible had it not been for his guidance. He turned the world of documentary sound on its head by introducing the 'gun' microphone and the Micron radio microphone into the game. The Micron remains today the finest radio microphone ever designed, and is a fitting legacy we have been left by Neville.

I knew him well, and sadly cannot thank him. Neville died in 1999.

I do thank his wife Beryl for taking me back to Audio

Engineering in January 1980, when I found walking on crutches particularly difficult. Beryl; you responded positively to the request from Brian and John, and I had an olive branch to lean on.

Mike Eley

It became clear quite soon why we had been mixed and matched to work on *Generations,* and I have to say it was a sensible choice. Luke was in prime condition to blend with the daughters, you were in good shape to bond with the mothers, and my stoop and breathless approach put the geriatrics at their ease (but I'll have you know I can still dress myself). Thanks for making that film such a pleasure to work on, as was the shoot in Botswana and the hunt for Lucan.

David Elliott

From the mid-1970s to the '80s, you and Jim Duffy edited some of our films and turned them from okay TV to 'By golly, that was a bit special' TV. The climax has to be the Tigris Expedition; I know Thor was pleased. Thanks for keeping my head above water and for the smooth track laying. You managed to make some of my dodgy stuff sound half decent!

David Graham

Thank you, thank you, thank you! If I didn't love you at first sight, I most certainly do now!

Most likely it began in Liverpool with the relatives of Tony Laryea, a family so remarkable it's become a memory I could never let go. I remember Ethel seeing you as a butterfly! This I had difficulty visualising, mainly, I think, due to your teeth. Then again, she did see me as an armadillo when on the dance floor, which is probably more accurate. She never did say what Martin was!

Apart from saving my life in the marshes of Southern Iraq, you became my security blanket on many other occasions.

The Omen – *A Bridge Too Far* – *Superman* – and others; this was the feature business, and I was out of my depth. You knew what was going on, not just because you had carried Robert Mitchum's bags in a movie, but because you just knew.

The Serengeti – Lake Rudolf – Amboseli – LA – Washington – Jerez de la Frontera – Sunday lunch with the Domecq's (how could I forget Sunday lunch with the Domecq's?) – a Vietcong magician – the banana split in Lesotho on Christmas Day – and so many more. You are a very special travelling companion.

For moving all my bits from the 'rubber room' to W13 with Rhiannon and Adam, for selling my car while I was abroad, for the numerous loaves of delicious bread that you baked (always eaten when still warm), for your generous nature and wonderful humour, for always being there when help was needed, and always for as long as it took; I thank you.

I feel that it is now long overdue, but I must offer an apology for sleeping on 'guard duty' whilst at Robinson's Island in 1974.

You exceptional friend – thank you with much love n' hugs.

Flora Gregory

Friendly, intelligent – a calm production manager with a sense of humour; sounds like a contradiction of terms. You, lady, are one, and not a hint of contradiction about you.

The entire crew were so glad you turned up on *Prisoner of Consciousness* and *Weather* – we needed much help and you always steered us in a sensible direction, never more so than on *Art, Faith and Vision*. I still enjoy seeing those films, made at a time when TV had stature and some credibility.

Thanks for including me on many good productions.

James Gray

Discovering a James Gray in northern Thailand is a most pleasing experience, and one to be recommended. When we finally caught the singing apes on camera and sound, I was particularly glad it was with you.

Not only do you make filming enjoyable, but you are a great 'bat wrangler'. I know the bat was only 6 inches from tip to tip, but if I'm on good form I can manage to tell a more harrowing tale with the bat up to 20 inches across and a fearsome set of dentures – I'm sure you understand.

Jo Hidderley

I guess the high spots have to be Jordan and the Black Sea, with Moscow and Leningrad coming in a close second.

I shall always be grateful to you for introducing me to the acceptable face of soft white flab on the beach at Aqaba. Since then sunbathing has become more of a comfort zone. Now you should see me strip off to my knitted swimwear with alacrity!

Thanks for the many hours of your company on some beautiful locations.

Iain Johnstone

A more precise and thoughtful line of questioning would be difficult to find anywhere. You are also the only director I have worked with on film who knew to within thirty seconds when a roll of film was about to finish. We did many good interviews, but the one at the top of the pile has to be with Marlon Brando on *Superman*.

Brando's people had only given you ten minutes: one magazine of film. An hour and fifteen minutes and seven rolls later, your skill and professionalism eased a superb interview from Mr Brando. So relaxed was he, that his people somehow forgot that Mr Brando had to be elsewhere and, as I'm sure you remember, he took us all for a meal. What an evening!

Stuart de Jong

Your editing always lets a film develop and breathe at the desired pace. You have edited many of the films I have worked on, particularly those directed by Taghi Amirani. Your timing and pacing of a film, linked with the use of music (or not), is exemplary. It's hardly surprising that many of Taghi's films have collected awards around the world. I remember sharing a room with you on locations in Zimbabwe, and I have to compliment you on the aim and trajectory of a shoe hurled the full length of the room at a four-inch cockroach – you seldom missed. The spiders, which were the size of large teacups, we gave the benefit of the doubt, as they could have had reinforcements.

I wish you and Sharon every happiness in Vancouver.

Tony Laryea

I had worked on a lot of five and ten-minute magazine programmes for the BBC and European Channels, but never on a full-length, fifty-minute BBC documentary. This all changed in 1973 when you took the three of us to Liverpool to meet part of your family. Who among us couldn't love them?

Apart from Liverpool being my all time favourite city in the UK, to discover people like Ray, Tina, Jasmin and Jason with their incorrigible mother Ethel, was almost too much for a Bradford lad.

It was wonderful to stay in the original Adelphi Hotel (long before corporate desecration) for three weeks while filming the epic. I know it was my first big one, and I was a bit overwhelmed at the time, but the strength and depth of the film remain and it is firmly placed in my top ten.

Thanks Tony, for inviting me to meet your family.

Martin Lightening

You're another of those rare 'listening' cameramen who are a pleasure to work with. The added bonus is that you not only like cricket, but actually *play* the game. Thanks for working on *Lady Guns* and the BBC's *Water* programme; these were memorable and enjoyable.

Jeremy Llewellyn-Jones

Where to begin? You have probably placed me in more emotional and overwhelming situations than any other director I have worked with. The children in *Cries of Alarm* brought more tears of joy and sadness than I can remember. Working with you and Chris at St Mary's on the Paediatric Wing gave us privileged access to the wonderful medical care performed in that unit, and a glimpse at the compassionate healing work done with the parents. I shall always be grateful to you for involving me in the work of Parviz Habibi and the team, fighting with all urgency and medical skill to overcome the monster of meningococcal septicaemia found in small children.

Travelling with Parvis and Chris in an ambulance at improbable speeds with the adrenaline pumping, willing us to arrive at the hospital in time to stabilize a child, is a memory I shall never lose.

It would be impossible to forget Winesha in Dallas or the gospel music we recorded at the church on Sunday.

Just when it looked like things were becoming tranquil, you hit us with Sioux City and the phenomenal people of that place – not only of the city, but the Sorensens of Alta on the farming plains of Iowa, and the discovery of Denny Fitch – what a remarkable man! Of all the unique and courageous people I have worked with, if I had to choose a hero from the past thirty-eight years, it would have to be Denny Fitch.

It is difficult to separate the magnitude of the medical films you have directed from the investigative approach to air accidents, leading to a further awareness of air safety, culminating in air traffic control in New York.

Near Miss will always be in the top five films of my work experience. You could only find a Dave Schoen in New York City – mothers just don't give birth to them anywhere else.

The key gift you possess – or maybe it's a skill, talent or natural instinct, probably a mixture of all of them – is your timing in asking *the* question. I don't mean your average question in an interview situation, but the questions you ask in a working/ actuality/ interview roll when under pressure. The doctors and nurses in the Intensive Care ward in Preston, and the air traffic controllers in New York were all under immense pressure and all responded well to you, because of the way you asked the question and the timing of its delivery. Simply put, I have never come across anyone better, and Ludovic Kennedy was good.

Thanks for letting me be part of it, not forgetting the shirt and the introduction to Sam Adams.

Harry Marshall

Art, Faith & Vision were very special films to have worked on. It's not every day of the week one bumps into Peter Levi and

Elizabeth Frink, but I think it was Cecil Collins who stole my affections. I keep meaning to call into the church in Basingstoke to have a look at the window, but of course I never do.

Introducing me to High Definition Television with NHK Japan and having a look at The Royal Collection with Christopher Lloyd is something for which I will always be grateful.

Never forgetting the remarkable NHK engineers, Makoto Taziri and Naohiro Yamamoto. When they said they would have to repair the camera in the field, they really meant in the field – and it was a muddy field – but they did, and it worked. I'll also never forget how much whisky they purchased at the Royal Distillery at Balmoral for their New Year celebrations in Tokyo. Some of those bottles were over £XXX.XX a bottle!

John Metcalfe

I remember John only with love and affection. In the winter of 1992 John and I visited twelve prisons and talked to some of the inmates who had contemplated or attempted suicide. John's understanding and empathy was immediately recognised by the prisoners, and a mutual bond of love and respect emerged between them.

I worked with John on many films and he was always good company to be with.

He died on Christmas Day 1994

Chris Morphet (the cameraman)

I may or may not get this correct, possibly I will. Chris Morphet; you are another man I found impossible to be with and not to love. You have a huge heart and a generous nature; you give your all and then give some more. Many directors have told me, 'Chris is fantastic/ brilliant/ incredible/ amazing…' Whichever one you go with simply reiterates his caring approach and generous heart.

Naturally, the influence of your Quaker education at Bootham in York would persuade you that most of the above is untrue and certainly questionable. So be it, but I could have a hundred people here within the hour to verify the opening paragraph.

None of this recognises your exceptional camera work,

especially the hand held work. But for me, the initial pleasure was to find a supreme craftsman who not only operated a camera but also listened. You always shoot the relevant dialogue at the right moment.

I fully appreciate that you may or may not agree, and could quite likely quote an example of indifferent camera work: on possibly one afternoon, maybe the second week in April 1982, probably the Thursday. This possibly, could also be true.

You also keep yourself in terrific condition. Swimming Olympic lengths at Gospel Oak Lido and cycling many miles when not working. I can only add; may your form of spiritual therapy at the cathedral of White Hart Lane where eleven disciples, (not of your choosing), continue to bring you excitement and pleasure – possibly.

I shall never forget your dogged determination to 'get the shot'. Others would have been in the bar, and on their second pint – not so with you, Chris.

One night at 3:30 a.m. in Camden Town, you and Maurice were being 'intrepid urban wildlife photographers' in the midst of a mini plague of rats. Not a rat was leaving the scene until they 'got into line'. It was all worth it; you got the shot, and Maurice registered pleasure.

Sharing your company has always been special, whether linked with individuals mowing lawns or repairing vacuum cleaners, air traffic controllers, nursing staff in Preston and Stoke, a small deaf child or a school in Leicester with remarkable teachers.

In seventeen years there have been many memorable occasions – too many to recount, but I know you remember them with affection, as I do.

I am aware that most of the above is possibly correct. However, it may or may not be found acceptable. Whatever the findings of the jury (who are still out), I know what I have written, and I know it is meant with love.

Carlo Muzi

Where to begin? The roads in Italy? The Twins? A&E in Stoke?

The Biennale in Venice – Damien Hurst – the boxing circuit in Tottenham – or literally heaving and rolling on the high seas off Scotland, and so many more. You were always there, keeping an eye on me as well as catering for Chris's every need on camera.

To select one incident is probably a bit futile, but I must: the mega trauma we had in the A&E at Stoke Hospital when we worked flat out through the night. You never missed a beat. You were always there with a fresh roll of tape as I ran out. You then stored all recorded rolls safely as well as changing lenses and magazines for Chris. It would be impossible to thank you sufficiently for the continual support you gave to me that night – I know I was on automatic for much of the time, but it worked.

I remember you looking at me as we wrapped the gear after the carnage; you smiled that wry smile, did your eyebrow thing, and said, 'Luther K – now that was trauma!'

I feel it would be impolite not to thank you quite openly for all the meals you ordered for me in Italy. Again, you never put a foot wrong, the food, although unknown to me, was always delicious. The speed of service always impressed me. Do you think your Roman accent was a key factor?

Thanks for your company and continual support, wherever the location.

Jill Nichols

To spend over a year at the RCA, on and off, was a treat beyond expectations. It turned out to be a privilege which has left a lasting memory with me. The talent and skill of the students together with their colourful imaginings was thrilling to be near. I clearly remember driving home on a real high on many of those evenings.

I think it was the freshness of their thinking and energy that gave me the boost. When I was at art school it was never like that; it was good to see what it could be.

Thanks for involving me in a unique experience.

Chris Openshaw

You absolutely spanking chap! I suppose one of the first things I noticed about you had to be the manner in which you worked. You must remember that on our first job in Malaysia you were quite a young sprog with a camera, and I was the resident geriatric-in-waiting.

I remember thinking after Sarah had introduced us, He's a bit young, but then I had to realise that almost everyone in the industry was a bit young. I also thought, He's very personable – I like him – I think.

After about twenty minutes of working on the first day with the orang-utans I realised that I *did* like you, and that developed into 'like a lot', but how could anyone that young be that good? I'd worked with many cameramen who were good, but they were older; they were supposed to be good.

The difference with you was that you were younger than they were, quite a bit younger than they were, but you were better. This isn't explainable – you just were.

As you have probably gathered, I was more than happy working with you then, and always have been on subsequent shoots.

I do thank you, along with Sarah, for introducing me to Booker T and the Monkeys – it seemed most appropriate at the time, and indeed still does. My kids thought it more than accurate, and occasionally use the reference to keep me in line.

I've seen a lot of your work since then and can only applaud. The work you have done recently is only to be expected from someone harnessing your talent. It was my privilege to be part of your working life then, and I continue to enjoy your work now.

Graham Paddon

When you have known someone from the age of twelve it is quite difficult to know how this is best handled. He probably knows more about me than I do about him.

As a boom swinger and sound assistant you pulled me through drama in Switzerland, as well as out of snowdrifts.

Thank goodness you turned up at the Royal Albert Hall to mix the sound for the documentary film with Cliff Richard. Without you, Tear Fund would have had a really quiet film!

I think we probably did our best work in Russia with Billy Joel. Despite the soaking in Red Square it was a terrific job, until your appendicitis kicked in.

Thanks for always turning up when most needed, always on time, always without a hangover, and for always being there when it most mattered. The salt of the earth could learn well from you.

I trust the cucumber sandwiches with the crusts cut off were to your satisfaction.

Michael Proudfoot

You are quite possibly the most eloquent, disciplined and considerate director yet, and still retain a sense of humour.

You know when you have got the material you require for your film, and I'm continually amazed at how quickly you get this. Again, you are still the only director I have worked with who consistently calls 'wrap' at 17:15, or thereabouts. More often than not we were back at the hotel, showered, shampooed, bouffed and polished by 18:30.

The friendly discipline you bring to a film is reflected in the final edit, which maintains a freshness on the second, fifth or however many viewings. *Classic Trucks* I still watch with much pleasure, not least for eating at the truck stop on Iowa State, Highway 80 – that is still the best apple pie and ice cream ever.

I do apologise for turning green whilst filming *Classic Ships* on the high seas off the Scottish coast. Despite being stretched out like a Viking and feeling wretched on that day, it was a wonderful series to work on. Thanks for giving me some of the most enjoyable work and company in thirty-eight years. The *Opera Workshop* you produced with Patrick has to be up among the good ones.

Fiona Reid

I first discovered the Fiona Reid experience with Taghi on *Earth Calling Basingstoke* – you have a warm, pleasantly unsettling nature made remarkable by your generosity. The memory still holds true.

It was soon discovered that you had the uncanny knack of doing the right thing, and then improving on it. As a production manager you were unusual by definition. On *Near Miss* with Jeremy, and many of Taghi's later films, you would always strike a fair deal with the crew. We had no complaints. We travelled comfortably and always safely. We were watered and fed satisfactorily, stayed in good hotels – we were happy chaps.

A couple of weeks after invoicing you for the job, you introduced a most peculiar set of rules. I would receive a polite phone call from you because you are a polite person.

'You can invoice me for more,' and you would then tell me by how much. Production managers from the mainstream gutter of television don't do this, but then you are not of that ilk.

I can only thank you for including me on many excellent productions that truly did shape my life.

Alan Root

Hanging around in trees with you cannot help but shape one's life. The experiences I listed in *Roots of Africa* would have told you a little about the changes you made in my life.

Possibly the later confrontations with Africa and nature have had a more lasting effect on me. I know filming the 'tribal wake' at night in the rainforest at Epulu in the Congo (Zaire), was unforgettable. The tropical deluge of warm rain at midnight was quite unbelievable, but I was there, I was drenched, it did happen.

The fifteen days following have left the most indelible memories, but the twelve-hour flight back to Nairobi in your Cessna, via Goma, Rwanda, Lake Victoria, the Serengeti, and Keekorok, is implanted forever. It was the most remarkable flight of my life, with Jenny waiting for us at your home.

You never did anything by halves, so when you asked me to live with you up a tree in the Central African Republic for ten days, it didn't seem unusual. When you also mentioned that due to the civil war we couldn't go immediately as there were bodies floating down the Sabah River and the missionaries had just left, this all seemed par for the course.

Sharing that experience with you and the photographer Alan Binks and being cared for by the pygmies is another rich privilege Africa shared with us.

I still have the 'home movie' you made at Epulu for Jenny, and wonder what became of that remarkable home in the rainforest. Jenny and you will always haunt my memory of the vast continent.

I shall always be grateful to you for sharing Africa with me, offering many golden moments to treasure.

Irwin Rosten

National Geographic knew what they were doing when they sent you to direct a film on the *River Thames* – apart from making a good film for them you took us to places on the river of which we were unaware.

Cricklade and Lechlade, the source of the Thames; Runnymede and sunrise over Eynsham. What about Churchill's War Rooms, long before they were open to general viewing? That was like going through a time warp.

Then those 'tasty' places we moored at near Henley and Wargrave. Did you realise that people like us don't get into places like that? But we were in. However did you get us into the Royal Windsor Horse Show with a film camera and sound, and then to the finishing line of the carriage and pair? Did you know the Duke of Edinburgh would win that event and be met by the Queen in raincoat, wellies and headscarf?

Irwin Rosten, you are one cool dude. It was a pleasure to have driven with you around Bucks, Oxon and Berks in '81. You take care, and many thanks.

Lucy Sandys-Winsch

I guess if I hadn't worked with you on any other film the *School Inspectors* would have to be one of the best. But then, your first one, *Memories in Store*, captured many wonderful moments. It was so disappointing for you that Chris was 'always in the wrong place – with the wrong exposure – and most of it was out of focus!' That was a tough day one for you, and we were supposed to be the crack team. What an induction! From there it was only natural that you would go from strength to strength – and you did.

School Inspectors is still in my top ten, and I sometimes think of those teachers under so much stress. You were very considerate in your handling of the staff and brought a degree of sanity and comfort to them in that terrible week. I believe it was game, set and match to you, with the Inspectors in a mediocre fourth place bringing up the rear. Teaching staff do not deserve to go through that emotional conflict; they have children to teach.

Your diplomacy was admirable.

The experience with the *School Inspectors* was a perfect training ground for *Paradise Island* – diplomacy, diplomacy, diplomacy. Well done, Lucy.

Peter Smith

I must, and always do, thank you for my introduction to the world of corporate films. I believe you and IBM covered my mortgage for at least six years.

The many fascinating trips we made to Rome, Spain, Italy, Holland, Germany and La Hulpe in Belgium. I think La Hulpe in 1982 was as close to a living sci-fi set as I have yet experienced.

I know it was your understanding of Italian culture and the language that got me a camera position in St Peter's Square no other cameraman came close to. I don't remember where Martin was, but he wasn't with us. All I remember is getting a close-up of the Pope giving his Sunday morning address to the thousands in the square with you recording the sound. We were good.

Today, things have changed quite a lot. I remember you said, 'The skill of production is to get the man with the wheelbarrow to come round the corner at 10:30 a.m.', and as far as I'm concerned, on your productions he always did.

Unfortunately, today the man with the wheelbarrow turns up at midday, if at all, and with a pushbike, and the crew have moved on to the next location.

Thanks for showing me discipline and skill in production.

Derek Taylor

You are one amazing man who saved my job so many times, in the '70s and '80s.

I have to thank you for taking me behind the scenes at the All England Tennis Club. This was a first for me, and having worked on interviews with John Newcombe, Ken Rosewall, Tony Roache and Kenny Fletcher is still a treasured moment in my tennis life.

I shall never know how you did it, but I am just pleased you did. I know I gave you interviews recorded with things like a vacuum cleaner in the next room; John Schlesinger for one – you may not remember, but I do.

When I gave you the recording of the interview there was a vacuum cleaner in the background. When you finished the transfer and passed it on to the film editor, I phoned the editor and apologised about the Hoover in the background; he simply said, 'What vacuum cleaner?'

You had a habit of doing this. I would give you recordings with extraneous noises on, and when the editor got the tracks to work with, the noises had gone. Thank you, thank you, thank you.

I suppose as far as I'm concerned your *pièce de résistance* came with *Streetwise*, a mere 200 plus rolls of sound transfer. All these rolls required careful transfer as they contained varying American accents, and you came through with fanfares and trumpets. When the Academy in Hollywood nominated *Streetwise* for a best sound award at the Oscars ceremony, it was down to you as much as it was down to me.

Thank you Derek, for your diligence, guidance and professionalism.

Forbes Taylor

That was a good bit of steering you performed at Lake Rudolf, with diplomacy to the fore in the presence of the competition.

Apart from scaring the living daylights out of me at first light by letting me know 'Africa screams', you were excellent company with which to share the heat and the Rudolf experience.

Thank you for providing me with the opportunity for such an adventure.

Adam de Wan

I don't know which to thank you for most – the Uden projects you gave me as a production manager, or the editing of many films I shot the sound for which you went on to mould, embellish and improve.

If I had to pick one moment which remains a lasting memory,

it would have to be filming the fisherman singing sea songs in that wonderful Cornish pub you guided us to. As pub singsongs go, they don't come much better.

I enjoyed working on the *Classic* series immensely, particularly the Cranes and Diggers, but then perhaps the Ms Wilson factor also played a prominent part.

I reckon the shaping and editing you managed to perform on the Eric Hebborn story was exemplary, despite the confusing circumstances. You produced a rewarding film for the BBC, and it remains with me as a good part of my life. Thanks Adam.

Reg Webb

I will always be grateful to you for your advice and guidance given to me over the years on radio microphones. Without doubt there have been many occasions when I would have come a technical cropper had you not pointed to a better way.

Until your wedding, the only thing I knew about Alberquerque was that it was there that 'Bugs Bunny knew he should have turned left'. It was kind of you and Laurie to invite me, and I remember with affection reading from Corinthians 13 for you both at the service. What an amazing wedding you had – my love to you both.

Susanna White

I suppose one ought not to be too surprised when you ask a healthy young Italian stud to remove all his clothes and get into the bath. After all, this is where you would like to film the interview. I know your mother would understand.

As usual he was pleased to oblige, and it was a good interview.

Your choice of documentary content is always interesting and often outstanding. One thing is for sure: they are entertaining, and prove to be good television. The added bonuses are the fascinating people discovered en route. Where else but in our business would you find a Simon, a Peter, a Gordon and a Gaynor, plus many other endearing people, not to mention dozens of Hassidic Jews?

Your films have been truly enjoyable work, and memorable

for many reasons. *Volvo City – Man Seeks Woman – Generations* – all offered much pleasure, but the one firmly in my top ten was your masterpiece on W H Auden. I believe you got as close as is possible on television to revealing Auden's relationships and his observation and understanding of love. I believe the poetry faculty at Oxford, along with Wystan, would have felt pleased that you had taken the time. I know I did.

Senara Wilson

Applause, applause, applause – you amazing, remarkable young woman! There simply isn't any way to open this that would be appropriate.

When we all met in New York on *Classic Trucks* it became evident within the first few minutes that you were different – you were very, very different. Your speed of thinking and humour, plus that cheeky, almost apologetic smile, left us very silent, reeling a bit, laughing and wondering.

We had been warned by the powers at Udens that, 'Senara is special – very special', but nobody mentioned in what way you were special. Someone had also told us, 'She is an Oxford graduate you know – a good one', no mention of a first, or a two one.

By the end of the first evening I knew why you were 'very special' – you contributed well to the production and saw humour in many situations, but it was a subtle, gentle humour wrapped in warmth and kindness.

Needless to say, during the rest of the shoot you were impeccable in everything you did, leaving the crew feeling they had each received special attention. I still don't know how you managed that.

I think Carlo could possibly be the only one with a question mark over that last paragraph. Did you really play Country and Western music loudly to him when he was driving you to the next location?

I remember towards the end of the week being in a lorry park waiting for a truck to turn up. The crew were chatting, but you had disappeared, only to reappear wearing a short skirt and white roller blades. To put it bluntly, I thought you looked terrific, and your cartwheels and acrobatics were worthy of an Olympic medal.

Undoubtedly, you were the 'Roller Blade Queen'.

A few years later it was good to learn you had been given some of the *Classic* series to film, and I was part of the team.

Chris and I anticipated that you would excel as a director, as you did with anything you put your mind to. Probably the most noticeable feature of your direction was the consideration and understanding you showed to the contributors.

All in all, you are pure joy to be with, and of course I love you – we all love you.

I'll sign off with a description of you I once heard; 'Senara is like an exploding super-nova in the dark firmament of television.'

John Wykes

I will always remember the help John gave me after I returned from Nairobi to London on crutches.

Working with Brian at Audio Engineering, they both constructed a gentle job for me at the light box, updating some of the artwork. This was perfect therapy for my somewhat battered body, and the medics at Barts Hospital were all for it.

John had worked with Neville Druce on the Micron radio microphone from the beginning. His knowledge of radio frequencies together with their working compatibility and legal requirements was second to none.

I am grateful for all the time John spent educating me in the best use of Micron technology, which proved so valuable on many productions over the years.

Tragically, John was killed in a car accident.